May you alway
your work.
lisbeth claus

#ZigZagHR

#ZigZagHR

WHY THE BEST HR IS NO LONGER HR

Lisbeth Claus — Lesley Arens

Lisbeth Claus & Lesley Arens, ZigZagHR: Why the best HR is no longer HR.
Global Immersion Press, 2019.
P.O. Box 1210, Silverton, OR 97381, USA.

This book is translated from the Dutch edition.
Lesley Arens & Lisbeth Claus, ZigZagHR: Waarom de beste HR geen HR meer is. Kalmthout, België: Pelckmans Pro, 2018.

Printed and distributed in the United Sates of America by Amazon.com
Cover design and layout: Jason Petz.

ISBN-13   978-0-9889329-4-4
ISBN-10   0-9889329-4-6

For permissions and speaking engagements, please contact the authors:
USA: lclaus@willamette.edu
EUROPE: lesley.arens@telenet.be

Content

Preamble to the English Translation

Although, Lisbeth Claus and Lesley Arens wrote the chapters of *#ZigZagHR* partially in both languages (Dutch and English), they decided to publish this book first in Dutch, rather than in English.

It was not really about the size of the market and target audience. Pelckmans Pro, our very supportive Belgian publisher, chose to only print 1,250 copies of the Dutch edition for its release in Belgium and the Netherlands. After all, the website of the World Federation of People Management Associations (WFPMA) lists 300 members of the PMClub in the Flemish part of Belgium, 4,200 members of the NVP in the Netherlands for the respective professional HR organizations in these Dutch-speaking countries. For us, it was a matter of pride. Lisbeth was born and raised in Belgium. Her postgraduate education and professional career took her to the United States and the world. Most of her professional and academic publications were in English (with only a handful in Dutch, French, German, or Spanish). Hence, she wanted her (perhaps) last and seventh book to be pubished first in one of her mother tongues.

The Belgo-Dutch HR practicing audience was also an incentive to start building the *#ZigZagHR*-Ecosystem (www.zigzaghr.be/nl) in these countries first. By doing so, they send the signal that not all progressive HR management practices cross the ocean in one direction. Despite a very rigid and complex legal and contractual employment environment, they found genuine excitement among HR practitioners in these small countries pioneering progressive HR practices. In many of their examples, they compared and contrasted HR policies and practices in both Belgium and Netherlands to the United States.

With subsequent translations, they want to send the *#ZigZagHR* message to the global HR community so large numbers of people—although many professionally competent in English—can read it in their own language with examples localized to their own context. We are dreaming big: look for localized translations in Portuguese, French, German, Spanish, Arabic, and Chinese soon!

Lisbeth Claus and Lesley Arens, March 29, 2019.

Preface to the Dutch Edition

BY LESLEY ARENS AND LISBETH CLAUS

> **Du choc des idées jaillit la lumière.**
> **(From the shock of ideas springs the light.)**
> Nicolas Boileau, 1636-1711

Lesley Arens (o1974) and Lisbeth Claus (o1951) are two women with very different trajectories who embarked on an international joint venture—writing a book about HR, as if the world needed another one!

These two Belgian *Straffe Madammen*, a term of endearment in Flanders for women who rock the boat, were first introduced virtually by a mutual colleague and friend Katrien Devos—the captain of HRbuilders. They consequently met face to face for the first time in May 2017. And, yes, things clicked in spite of their differences.

Lesley is younger, lives in Belgium; is impulsive and daring; is an exuberant networker full of fertile ideas; planting them without much concern for their viability; is sometimes a bit of a procrastinator, tending to rely on intuition; and is not really in HR. Lisbeth is older (way past retirement age according to Belgian norms); lives in the Pacific Northwest of the United States; is planned and deliberate; has a life-long HR career in industry and academia; is more likely to use reasoning; and embraces new ideas but scrutinizes them for research-based evidence and whether they can be implemented and made to stick. Lesley loves to use English expressions in her speaking and writing, while Lisbeth uses either English or Dutch. Both have a passion for innovation and breaking the mold. *#ZigZagHR* is the result of their clashing ideas and the many transatlantic discussions engendered over the past year.

Despite their differences, they strongly agree the 21st century context of work and the worker requires us to walk away from traditional HR and rethink its current policies, practices, and structures. While traditional HR was good in the past and has served us well, it no longer works today and will definitely not in the future! This holds true in both Belgium and the United States. Although our minds may be ready for rethinking the traditional HR model, our policies, practices, and (especially Belgian) structures are not prepared. The essence of *#ZigZagHR* explores new ways of thinking and doing in HR—we are not blowing up our bridges, but we must change and *#ZigZag*. HR change must be rooted in action. Even if the progressive HR framework is vague and uncertain today, we must figure out which HR best serves our purpose in this new context. The values and norms of the workforce are evolving. So should HR!

What a journey the writing of this book has been! An academic writes in footnotes, a creative generalist in prose. Lisbeth writes predominantly in English, while Lesley writes in Dutch. In *#ZigZagHR*, they envision a continuum with two extremes and HR must *#ZigZag* in between. As a matter of fact, both Lisbeth and Lesley are also on a continuum and find themselves at extremes. This has proven to be their major strength.

This book would not have been possible without their personal contradictions and the strong ecosystem they have built as professional women around the world. Many thinkers and doers have impacted their ideas and the progressive practices they embrace. They decided to write this book on how careers can be different, will and have to change, and what that means in concrete terms for HR.

Lesley and Lisbeth believe there has never been a better time to be in people management as HR (or whatever we choose to call it) is one of the most progressive places to be in an organization today.

Lesley Arens, Oudenaarde, East-Flanders (Belgium).
Lisbeth Claus, Silverton, Oregon (USA).
October 9, 2018.

Introduction

WHY WE WROTE *#ZIGZAGHR*

> **The voyage of the best ship is a zigzag line of a hundred tacks.**
> Ralph Waldo Emerson

#ZigZag: a set of Z shaped, meandering lines; angled; a movement of a line abruptly taking one or more sharp changes of course; a broken line that goes back and forth and has sharp corners.

#ZigZagHR offers a more robust and sustainable answer to what the workforce of today and tomorrow expects and needs in a rapidly changing world of work. Later in this book we introduce a set of competencies—many from other management disciplines—that HR must develop and adopt to respond to the expectations and to bridge the gap between what HR offers today and what is expected from HR.

And, we dare ask the question out loud, whether the current—even best—HR practices of today will still be here tomorrow?

#ZigZagHR is not a plea for tabula rasa. Besides, that is also impossible for most companies—with the exception of start-ups who do not carry along the "mess of the past" (MOP). Perhaps we should refer to it more appropriately as the "shit of yesterday" (SOY), with a grateful wink to the model that Peter Hinssen developed in his book, *The Day After Tomorrow*.[1]

#ZigZagHR wants to paint a picture to organizations, employers and, most importantly HR that communicates traditional HR is no longer sufficient and must evolve with an extra dimension to become what we describe as "progressive HR." This new HR must focus on the entire workforce instead of just the core employees (*#ZigZagHR-*Workforce). The new HR must focus on the value it can bring (*#ZigZagHR-*Careers) and the new HR needs to develop a set of competencies parallel and complementary to the current HR-competency profile (*#ZigZagHR-*Stack). Finally, we must aim to create a new form of HR operations (*#ZigZagHR-*Operations).

This book is different #WhatDidYouthink. It proposes a framework to reinvent HR for organizations who simply cannot start over because of their legacy. It also proposes a set of tools that employers can adopt to experiment with more progressive practices. We strive to be a sounding board for a do-it-yourself *#ZigZagHR* innovations through an engaged online and offline network of HR professionals. We want to build, together with you, a new *#ZigZagHR-*Ecosystem of progressive HR leaders who continuously learn best and next practices and share experiences.

If HR wants to be agile and relevant, we must augment the traditional HR function with progressive *#ZigZagHR* thinking.

For years already we have been looking over the wall for best, leading, and next practices in HR. And what we realized very clearly during the writing of this book is that:

1. It is a good time to be in HR.
2. *#ZigZagging* is the key to success in "The Future of Work."
3. We must look to the outside: literally and figuratively, outside of our HR-silos, outside of our comfort zone, outside of the walls of our own organization.

Not only are our personalities as authors of this book very different, our careers are divergent and anything but linear.

Lisbeth started out as a medical sociologist and took an academic route at Belgian and American universities. Then, she stepped into the business world, where she was active as a consultant and held HR management functions for Fortune 50 companies. She traveled the world as a global HR consultant and landed back in academia as a management/global HR professor for the training of MBAs.

Lesley started her career in adult education when she put down the importance of life-long learning as Managing Director of the East-Flemish Consortium for adult education in Belgium. Fourteen years later, she became the director of a federation for HR learning and professionals. The last two years she has been at HRbuilders, an HR-interim-management provider and market leader in Belgium. She has a dual role. As a business partner, she matches HR freelancers and connects them internationally with employers who need temporary HR services. As a marketeer, she is responsible for all content, social media and client HR events. With her own company under the umbrella of "Connect & Learn," she organizes exclusive and original network events on leadership, life-long learning, and HR.

We always knew very well where we were headed and saw every career detour as an opportunity. And because it was very clear what we wanted (and didn't want), we *#ZigZagged* throughout our careers toward where we are today with a definite red thread: we look at things with a fundamentally different set of glasses, we tend to see and observe things that others often don't, and we know how to connect the dots. Authors call this the behavior of mavericks and non-conformists. We call it *#ZigZagging*! This image is the basic idea of this HR book.

#ZigZag:

a set of Z shaped, meandering lines;

angled;

a movement of a line abruptly

taking one or more sharp changes

of course;

a broken line that goes back and

forth and has sharp corners.

1

Why #ZigZagHR

A NEW WORLD, A NEW HR

1

In chapter 1, we sketch the context in which HR operates today and explain why we push *#ZigZagHR* as an alternative model to the current talent management and HR policies and practices. We have reached the fourth industrial revolution where the customer and employee experience are central, and where demographic and technological developments and globalization have an unmistakable impact on work and the worker. This new reality offers the momentum and opportunity to reinvent talent management. This first chapter is actually the ultimate wake-up-call.

#The future of work does not scare us!

The 586 million hits on Google at the end of January 2018 deliver the irrefutable proof that #The Future of Work is a buzzword. British professor Lynda Gratton (London Business School) mapped out the trends that have an impact on the total workforce in her many years of research. Gratton pleads for a fundamental change in the way we think about work. In *The Shift: The Future of Work is Already Here* (2011),[2] she describes the five dynamics that, according to her research, strongly influence the way we will work in the future: technology, globalization, demography (in combination with a longer life expectancy toward 100 years), social changes, and energy consumptions. Her book gives a number of default scenarios that are worth (re)reading today. In addition, she describes three shifts, three fundamental transformations that we must go through to be successful in the future world of work:

- **FROM GENERALIST TO SERIAL SPECIALIST:** It is no longer sufficient to be a specialist in one particular discipline, because no single domain can last for a life-long career. By 2025, no single (!) job will look the same as today. That means that even specialists must continuously learn other domains. We write about this extensively in chapter 3: *#ZigZagHR*-Workforce.
- **FROM ISOLATED COMPETITION TO INNOVATIVE COOPERATION:** The future is no longer made up of individuals who—using elbow grease—push themselves to the top. The future now belongs to the networked top performer who can play several roles, work with others, and add value.
- **FROM CONSUMER TO PASSIONATE PRODUCER:** Where meaningful work done well is more important than the amount of money in one's bank account at the end of the month.

The books, blogs and podcasts of Jacob Morgan offer inspiration to anticipate the changes in how we work. In *The Future of Work* (2014),[3] Morgan describes how we will work differently in the future and the impact this has on how we manage and lead. In his more recent book, *The Employee Experience Advantage* (2017),[4] he describes the importance of experiences of employees and how one concretely binds employees by together focusing on the physical, cultural and technological aspects of the work environment.

According to Josh Bersin, "the future of work" is already a reality today and that should not scare us. In his article, "The Future Of Work: It's Already Here—And Not As Scary As You Think" (*Forbes*, 2016), he sketches the impact of the new work reality at the individual worker, the organization and societal levels.[5] At a personal level, the new work reality is about why we work (meaning), how we work and how we integrate work into our lives, how our career evolves, and how we can keep our competencies up to date. At the organizational level, the new work reality is about which kind of jobs there will (and won't) be in the future, what the added value is of people in an automated digital world, and how we can engage workers in a flexible manner to meet the demands of the ever rapidly changing context. Finally at the societal level, the new work reality is about how we as a society can (re)educate people, prepare and support them in their many transitions; it is also about which societal challenges we are facing such as migration, income disparities, and unemployment.

#Imagine... A future worker applies for a job without a resume or curriculum vitae and is hired without being interviewed by a person. Smart algorithms predict who is likely to leave your company and when; chatbots answer HR generalist questions; employees have total flexibility as to when and where they work and have unlimited paid time off!

What today is considered a revolutionary trend or weird practices in HR is perhaps next year's leading practice.

In reality, for progressive employers, the future of HR is already here and constantly evolving.[6]

More than ever,

HR can prove its added value

by letting people and organizations

flourish in this new world.

But that requires a new HR.

A *#ZigZagHR*.

Harder, better, faster, stronger

"Work it harder—Make it better—Do it faster—Makes us stronger," are the words we hear from Daft Punk, the helmeted French electrovirtuosos. Their song perfectly fits the current situation of HR. Or not? When looking at the numbers and comparing it with the past, the speed seems to be perception rather than reality. But perception *is* reality and ensures that people experience the current developments as faster, more drastic, and even more terrifying.

VUCA is another unavoidable buzzword—and we promise solemnly that we will use it as least as possible in the following chapters—an acronym originating in the military environment of the U.S. Army War College at the turn of the 21st century and, in the meantime, part of the management vocabulary.[7] It stands for Volatility, Uncertainty, Complexity, and Ambiguity. If everything changes continuously and rapidly, if everything is uncertain, complex, and vague, it forces us to work in a different manner. Bob Johansen of the California non-profit research Institute For The Future (IFTF) describes the new VUCA-leadership competencies as follows: Vision, Understanding, Clarity, Agility. According to him, it comes down to listening through the noise and not accepting the future as a fixed given.[8]

Speed is no longer an option, but a must. And even more than speed, it is about agility, according to the Belgian entrepreneur and author Peter Hinssen. In his book, *The Day After Tomorrow*, he proposes an answer to the VUCA environment and summarizes it as VACINE, meaning Velocity, Agility, Creativity, Innovation, Networks, and Experimentation.[9] It comes down to detect the changes in a timely manner, to estimate the possible impact quickly and correctly, and preferably anticipate and tirelessly search for opportunities these changes bring with them.

> # The underlying message is to view the turbulence as an opportunity rather than a calamity. This implies employees and management must be ready to look at their work challenges as an opportunity.

Welcome to the fourth Industrial Revolution

In the last 200 years, employers have shifted their focus a few times with regard to their employees. During the first industrial revolution, the focus was on utility: what do people need to do their job? During the second industrial revolution, the focus shifted to productivity: what do people need to do their work as efficiently as possible? During the third industrial revolution, the attention went to engagement: how can people become more engaged at work so productivity increases and employees gain? We haven't quite achieved that since engagement and productivity are relatively low and workers are disengaging and dropping out either mentally, physically, or a combination of both.

> **Anno 2018, we have landed in the fourth industrial revolution and everything is focused on the employee experience.[10]**

Today engagement is all about the employee experience or in other words: how do we create the ultimate experience for our employees (and workers) and how do we create that concrete form in the workplace so employees want to show up and make an effective contribution. It is rather sobering that companies invest a lot of time, money, and energy in the creation of the ultimate (external) customer experience, but do not seem to translate that in the internal (customer) experience of their employees. That's not only unfortunate, but also has far away consequences for operating results.

> **The most important drivers of the fourth industrial revolution in which we currently reside are demography, technology, and globalization.**

DEMOGRAPHY: WE WILL LIVE LONGER, WE WILL WORK LONGER!

People live longer and work longer, or that is at least the intent—this does not seem to work as well in Belgium compared to other European countries and the United States. The fact that Belgians want to leave the workforce as quickly as possible and still continue to leave in droves is in sharp contrast with the work ethic in the United States, where babyboomers who lose their jobs in their fifties and sixties simply start again, often in lower paying jobs. This is partially because American society does not have a social safety net compared to most European countries. Also, among the babyboomers in the U.S. more of a #YesWeCan (or is it #WeHaveNoChoice) mentality and work—especially knowledge work—is synonymous with having a meaningful life. Whereas in Belgium, people and politicians engage in endless debates and negotiations for allowing early retirement for a long list of heavy occupations (called *zware beroepen* in Dutch).

Currently, there are four generations working together on the floor. This represents great challenges according to *The 100-Year Life: Living and Working in an Age of Longevity* (2016), which pointed out that one needs more money when one lives longer. This means working longer (even into our seventies or eighties and that is possible because we likely will stay younger longer), or living with less, or saving more and working longer than we really want or are able.[11]

TECHNOLOGY: BRAVE NEW DIGITAL WORLD, ROBOTS ON THE RISE

Big data and the Internet of Things (IoT) are the new gold, not just in companies, but also in daily life where digital developments succeed each other at a dizzying tempo. Technology, especially developments in artificial intelligence, machine learning, and deep learning, has an unmistakeable impact on work. On one hand, many jobs people are currently working risk being replaced by robots and computers; it is an economic reality that employers want to get work done in the most cost efficient manner. Computers, robots, and machines don't tire out, don't get sick, don't get pregnant and don't take vacations. They make rational decisions based on algorithms and are, therefore, less susceptible to the unconscious biases of people. On the other hand, many tasks still will need to be done by people. Think about anything that has to do with empathy, creativity and innovation. The fact that people will be freed from certain tasks, more time will be made for HR to focus on the bridge function between what employees want and the objectives of organizations. This function is a lot more strategic than the transactional HR functions that absorb our time every day.

> # Nobody can predict what this brave new digital world will bring, no one knows what it will bring, and where the labor market will be impacted the most and the fastest. However, it will definitely have great consequences for HR, for its stakeholders (employees, managers, unions, and stockholders), and what will be expected from HR. What is striking is the fact that most companies who are busy with the digital transformation, HR is hardly involved.

GLOBALIZATION: THINK GLOBAL, ACT LOCAL

Because of globalization, labor has become more accessible across borders and also cheaper; employers in Belgium must now compete with companies in countries where taxation and social security are a completely different story. In Europe and the U.S., the pendulum has swung completely in the other direction toward protectionism and anti-globalization (Brexit, Trump). Work may have become more accessible and cheaper, but it is unfortunately coupled with growing inequality, an increasing gap between the haves and have nots, and growing un(der)employment, especially among younger workers. This creates big challenges for HR in Belgium in terms of legal regulations in the different countries, localization of HR practices, and the growing diversity of teams in the workplace. American and European employers have difficulty finding employees with the right competencies and engagement. In the U.S. for example, Amazon is looking for 500.000 (!) extra workers to support its expansion over the next five years. For HR, this means more and more that talent management must cross the borders and use different recruiting and selection methods to fill its vacancies.

Disruption

These transformations at the macro level (demography, technology, and globalization) have a drastic impact on the labor market and the actors who are active in it. The challenges of companies today, tomorrow, and the day after tomorrow cannot be compared with the challenges of yesterday. Fast changing technologies, a complex market with extremely competitive pressures due to more demanding and less loyal customers, and the disruption of many industries make it necessary for companies to set themselves up as agile and sustainable.

> # The fourth industrial revolution not only creates a revolution in work and the worker, but also in HR and talent management. This new reality of the context of work, the way we work, the way we want to work, where we work, and who works are fundamentally changing and will continue to do so.

We expect people to be always-on, continuously update their competencies, reinvent their job, and take their career in their own hands. Leaders and managers are expected to support their teams during these transitions and create a chain of positive experiences in this multicultural new reality where transformation continue to follow each other at a rapid pace. And the social partners look argus-eyed at these developments. The social consultation process in Belgium is traditionally based on a conflict model: the helpless employee must be protected against the malicious employer. Companies who want to bet on the long term are doomed in advance if they get into a heated consultation with the unions who mainly serve short-term needs. Consequence: a restless social climate with gray compromises and bought off social peace, where employers see social elections as a necessary evil that they must face rather than an opportunity to have a true dialogue in favor of all involved. In the

U.S., the gap between the top 0.1% (super rich) and the 9.9% (knowledge workers who are employed and serve the 0.1%) and the bottom 90% (the rest of the working and non-working population who hardly are considered in terms of education, income, healthcare, and social mobility) is increasing. The 10% of super rich and knowledge workers are now labeled the "new aristocracy."[12]

> #It is very painful to acknowledge that current HR (and talent management) has, up to now, not given a conclusive and compelling answer to respond to this fundamentally changed context: through rigid, functional job descriptions and inflexible structures, organizations continue to chase the facts in a status-quo mode, stay in a conflict mode, and workers are more and more checking out mentally and/or physically.

In 2018, Belgium reached a discouraging record of an ever-increasing number of people who are no longer active on the labor market due to long-term illness (5% of the active population between the ages of 20 and 64) and burn-out (with the strongest in the age category 30 to 40 years, where almost 21% feels emotionally tired and burn-out is around the corner). The rapid rate of increase of the non-active workforce is especially worrisome: in four years the number of long-term illness in Belgium rose by 22%, where psychosocial conditions are playing a considerable role.[13] In the meantime, everyone points the finger at the other, while people who are employed pay a bill that gets more expensive by the day.

This is in stark contrast with the U.S.,where progressive talent management practices are dictated, on one hand, by powerful mega employers (like Amazon, Facebook, Starbucks and Microsoft) and, on the other hand, by small (less than 500 employees) flexible start-ups (mostly in IT),while the rest of the (small, medium or large) companies still run in a traditional HR harness.

Mind the gap

It is clear the solutions for the challenges described above are complex and interventions will have to be made at three different levels: the individual, the employer, and the society. HR can and must play a leading role as a forerunner. HR is still too much caught between the expectations and needs of the employees and the priorities of the employer, failing to offer a compelling answer to either one.

The "average" employee in Belgium still strives for security and stability, preferably under the form of a fixed employment contract: in 2015, labor mobility in Belgium reached an absolute low of 5%.[14] With "labor mobility" we mean the extent that people change employers, careers, or region in the labor market. The more people change jobs, careers, or region, the larger the mobility. Despite the fact that in the year 2018, Belgian professionals dared to change jobs and take on a hybrid status more often than a fixed contract, the majority of workers are still determined to have a traditional standard labor contract, as do others in most of Europe. In contrast, in the U.S., people often change work every two years, since job security has already long ago been replaced with work security and finding a meaningful job is seen as an individual responsibility. It is hard to blame the Belgian worker for basically remaining so status-quo oriented (i.e., the golden cage principle). They are culturally brought up to be risk averse and taking matters into one's own hands was strongly frowned upon. Perhaps this trend will shift as the babyboomer generation will ultimately leave the labor market. However, the idea that older workers strive for security and younger workers do not is obsolete. Several studies show us the facts: in Belgium young people too still strive for security.[15]

> **# Considering that many jobs will disappear or will fundamentally change in content at a faster tempo, it is clear that only agile organizations will survive this disruption.**

These agile organizations are looking for employees with career resilience. By career resiliency, we mean the extent to which workers take initiative to take their careers in their own hands and consciously plan the next step(s) of their work future. This implies a deeper and bigger gap between jobs with greater autonomy and those with little or no empowerment, which became the difference between attractive and unattractive jobs. This leads to "job polarization," as economist Alan Manning calls it, with the disappearance of middle-class jobs.[16]

Those who fail to take their careers in their own hands and those whose current jobs are based on repetitive or manual processes will, to a large extent, see their jobs disappear. When entering a railway station in Belgium, think about the employees at the ticket counter. They will mostly be replaced by automatic ticket machines, while the checkers at American supermarkets will be replaced by self-check-out machines.

It is crystal clear the solutions for these challenges are complex and interventions must happen at three different levels: individual, employer, and society. HR can and must play a leading role during this transformation.

How long do I need the talent (and HR)?

Companies are shouting from the roof top that their employees are their most valuable resource, but in reality they focus on savings in their labor costs. In this volatile, uncertain, and global context, the market demand for labor is unpredictable. Therefore, companies have to be agile enough to respond to these external changes. They can do this best when they are able to build a flexible shell around their fixed core of talent. Peter Cappelli sees the "make versus buy" decision in talent management—a balance between employee and contractor status—as a solution to reduce the uncertainty of the demand for talent in the workforce supply chain. The balance is contingent upon the answer to those four questions:[17]

1. How long do I need this talent?
2. How accurate is my forecast?
3. Is there a hierarchy of competencies based on their importance?
4. How important is it to preserve my current organizational culture?

We must accept that organizations need to build in more flexibility not only because they desire to do so as part of their thought-out strategy, but also because the context forces them to change. The new solutions often demand other competencies within the organization that are currently neither present nor visible. While some of these competencies might actually be in the organization, they are not in the existing delineated job descriptions and profiles.

In short, we must learn to live, survive, and reinvent ourselves in this "new normal" reality. We must accept that the careers of the future will continue to transform, sometimes very brusquely.

Trends in the U.S. and Europe clearly show the number of freelancers and contract workers with a hybrid status will only increase.[18] For the individual worker, life- or career-long learning is the basic condition to defy the disruption and to survive.

Almost a half a century ago, the American railway magnate Alfred Edward Perlman predicted: "Learning is what most adults will do for a living in the 21st century." His prediction has come through today. Professor Frederik Anseel, researcher Lien Vossaert, and HR experts David Ducheyne and Frank Vander Sijpe suggest in their Dutch 2018 book, *Personaliseren van Werk—Mythes & Feiten* (Personalization of Work: Myths and Facts) we have to abandon the illusion of job security and evolve to work security. There will always be work throughout people's careers; they will not only need to want, but also be able to engage in different roles.[19]

The glasses make the difference

We predict with conviction that in the near future, half of what HR does in terms of transactions will be automated and that 80% of what HR people do today, they will no longer be doing in the near future. This near future is the next two to five years. Due to different technological developments, computers, and robots will perform many jobs more efficiently and productively.

There are two ways to look at this new reality: with a negative lens where one sees a fateful dystopia with an unemployed society, an unbridgeable gap between the haves and the have nots, between well paying and miserable jobs, and HR limited to transactional activities. With a positive lens, the focus is on opportunities: if 80% of the administrative and routine HR tasks are automated and taken over by algorithms, it frees up time for HR to focus on people activities where HR is better than computers. If 80% of HR's daily tactical tasks are no longer relevant, it frees up time to support tasks that have greater strategical value. Because of technology, we are able to make better data-driven (read: evidence-based) decisions. We can personalize HR and bring the H back in HR.[20]

HR, this is your ultimate wake-up call

Too many HR practitioners are still convinced things will not take this route. They don't deny the world is changing drastically, but they are not convinced they will be affected or they are not agile enough to react to the situation change. Perhaps this is a healthy overdose of self confidence or awkward hubris! Peter Hinssen calls this *Eisenbahnscheinbewegung*, referring to the fake feeling one gets in a stationary train when the train on the next track starts moving. The brain thinks one is moving and the other train is standing still while in fact the opposite is true.[21]

The HR functions as we still know it in many organizations today are at the point of becoming obsolete, unless HR can reinvent itself and make its added value concrete. HR must not only redefine its "talent value proposition," but also propose an alternative model that provides a conclusive answer while searching for competencies it does not yet have. The current siloed HR thinking must make place for networks and the building of communities of interests in- and outside the company. In lieu of being a CHRO (Chief HR Officer), HR must play (and demand) the role of CAO (Chief Adaptability Officer) between the employer and the workforce, and even better become the architect of the employee experience.

Although many companies are moving towards becoming extremely customer focused, this is not yet the case for the internal customer: their workforce (whether these are people on the payroll, freelancers, contractors or gig-workers). HR does not operate totally yet from a customer orientation, but still too much from its processes, policies and procedures that make live easier for HR.

> Therefore, we make a plea for a new *#ZigZagHR*-Architecture and a corresponding *#ZigZagHR*-Stack parallel to the existing HR that will prepare HR better for tomorrow and the day after tomorrow.

We must make strategic decisions regarding: which activities we will continue to do in the future because they are the core of HR; which activities we better stop because they no longer add value and which new activities we must introduce because they are innovative and important. With *#ZigZagHR*, we propose a new HR-framework and architecture that every company can adopt: small or large, domestic or international, traditional or progressive.

The real HR story does not necessarily come from Silicon Valley, Seattle, London, or a gigantic global company. It is being written on the workfloor of engaged, agile and progressive HR teams in companies in Roeselare, Belgium or Birmingham, Alabama.

Progressive companies (as we like to call them) understand the current talent management practices no longer suffice. Progressive companies understand talent management is customized (one size will never fit all), while at the same time it complies with the legal requirements. Progressive companies know the only way to get there is by creating an employee experience and taking into account the needs and requirements of their stakeholders. Progressive companies actively look for non-conformists and *#ZigZagHR*-Profiles that have a new set of competencies that are complementary to the existing HR-Competencies.

Our #ZigZagHR model has four anchors that we will briefly review in the next chapter and describe in greater detail in the subsequent chapters:

- **#ZigZagHR-Workforce**
- **#ZigZagHR-Stack**
- **#ZigZagHR-Careers**
- **#ZigZagHR-Operations**

IN SUMMARY

The fourth industrial revolution that we are currently experiencing—driven by changes in demography, technology, and globalization—has an unmistakable impact on work and the worker. This new reality offers the momentum for HR to reinvent talent management and enhance and enrich the ultimate "sweet spot" where what is good for the employer is also good for the employees. This first chapter is your wake-up call to adopt the #ZigZagHR model that we will elaborate on in the next few chapters.

2

The #ZigZagHR Model

BECAUSE HR MUST (DARE-WANT-MAY-CAN) COLOR OUTSIDE OF THE LINES

2

For years HR has worked hard to conquer a seat at the table, but has not really been able to adapt to the (rapidly) changing times and needs. Hence, the HR bashing continues. Instead of being defensive and complain about what holds us back, we should build on the progress we have made so far. In any case, a fundamental metamorphosis is urgently desired and that does not happen with a tabula rasa but by *#ZigZagging* strategically. In this chapter, we introduce the *#ZigZagHR*-Model with its four anchors: *#ZigZagHR—Workforce*, *#ZigZagHR—Stack*, *#ZigZagHR—Careers*, and *#ZigZagHR—Operations*.

HR in a quagmire

Born in the Northern hemisphere with a strong Anglo-Saxon bent, HR developed during the first decades of the 20th century from the need of employers to have an administrative personnel function inside the organization to comply with the emerging labor laws. It solidified in the US context with the application of psychological selection tests after World War II. The early "personnel" function took on a compliance role and focused mainly on transactional personnel activities. The HR administrative function mirrored the industrial model of organizations of the time.

Decades later, with the advent of the post-industrial society, the call for HR to become more strategic and "having a seat at the table" ultimately led to an expanding talent management role. Yet, in spite of professionalization efforts, the contribution of HR as a value-added management function has never been fully been recognized and largely ignored by the executive C-suite.

The love-hate relationship with HR

Over the years, there has been a fair amount of criticism of HR—both from within and outside HR—for not being relevant. It led to a love-hate relationship with HR. Outsiders expressed their hatred for HR, while insiders struggled to justify their people management contributions. In a now legendary article, "Why We Hate HR," in *Fast Company* (August 2005), Keith H. Hammonds asserted that after 20 years of talking about being strategic partners, most HR people are neither strategic nor leaders. The reasons enumerated are numerous: the people pursuing HR careers aren't necessarily the best and the brightest; HR pursues efficiency in lieu of value; HR isn't working for employees; and the C-suite does not get HR (and vice versa).[23]

A decade later, Peter Cappelli's article, "Why We Love to Hate HR…and What HR Can Do About It," in the *Harvard Business Review* (July-August 2015)[24] reported that the complaints about the HR function are driven by the business context (namely the supply and demand of labor) and that HR managers focus too much on *administrativia* and lack vision and strategic insight. He proposes a number of solutions: rethink programs that have been around since the 1950s; make a business case for initiatives that matter; and cut loose pet programs that lack impact.

In a previous *Harvard Business Review* article, "It's Time to Split HR," (July-August 2014) Ram Charan et al. suggest that the CHRO (Chief HR Officer) can become a true strategic partner by predicting outcomes, diagnosing problems, and prescribing actions on the people side that will add value.[25]

These controversies about HR's role and value are augmented by the general lack of professionalization of HR. People without formal HR background (university training or other credentials) often find themselves in HR roles by serendipity rather than choice. With or without training or a set competency profile, HR is open to anyone who can and wants to do it. In spite of the rise of specialized university HR programs, the growth of HR professional organizations around the world and the growing trends towards certification (especially in the UK and the US), the threshold for entering the profession remains.

Arguably, the existing preparation for the HR métier today (whether through university education or professional training and socialization), is in need of reinvention. The educational models are too often based on past thinking, showing a tremendous HR research-practice gap[26] and tending to lag in their approach for dealing with the new world of work and the worker.

In addition, it is not easy to determine when HR is successful because the critical success factor for HR practice are poorly described in comparison with other management disciplines such as marketing, accounting, finance, and operations.

So "over and out" with HR?

Of course not!
In spite of continued HR bashing, one thing most people agree with is the ability to attract the best and brightest people, keeping them engaged with a company, and allowing them to innovate is key to organizational success. While most companies have access to similar tools and systems, the only differentiating factors they can count on are their people's engagement and the culture of innovation they create.

Start-up companies understand that all too well and capitalize on the power of their people often without having HR in the starting block. Only when they get a critical mass of employees do they structure some form of people management practices around their culture. In many of these progressive organizations, there are individuals, groups, and networks that are advocating and experimenting with innovative and progressive HR practices and show a passion for the value of people management. They are outside of mainstream HR, however, and tend to put a distance between themselves and the HR label—they show that the best HR is perhaps no longer HR!

About dinosaurs and boxes...

HR is not immune to the disruptive forces of innovation of demography, information technology, and globalization we described in the previous chapter, especially when its practices are based on a 20th century organizational business model. Automation and artificial intelligence will (and already has) takeover many of the HR transactional activities that today are performed by HR generalists, but HR specialists will not get away with it either.

If HR cannot adapt to the changing context of the fourth industrial revolution, it could go the way of the dinosaurs even earlier than we currently can (or dare to) imagine.

> **To remain relevant, HR must learn to color outside of the lines and embrace innovation in the form of new ways of thinking and acting.**

There is no doubt that HR is in need of reinvention. We are not just talking about adopting the latest fad that comes along, reaffirming our seat at the table, partnering with the business but forgetting the workforce customer (and vice versa), making incremental improvement or any other cosmetic change. This would simply only mean that we rearrange the deck chairs on the Titanic! But how can HR truly be transformed to meet the current and future needs of work and the worker?

One approach that has been suggested for transforming organizations and boosting innovation is the "three-box" approach. In Vijay Govindarajan and Christ Trimble's article from the *Harvard Business Review*, "The CEO's Role in Business Model Reinvention,"[27] they use a three-box solution strategy for leading innovation: box 1 represents the activities that improve the performance of day-to-day business; box 2 deals with the need to overcome the dominant logic of the ways business is done currently; and box 3 relates to things that are truly innovative and can change the business.

> # Applied to HR in our organizations, the three-box model requires us to manage the current HR activities required for the business in terms of legal compliance and value-added activities (box 1), selectively abandon the HR activities of the past that no longer add value (box 2), and create innovative practices for the future (box 3).

In chapter seven, we zoom in on the concept of "the three boxes" and elaborate on what this means concretely for HR.

It's the culture, stupid?

In reinventing HR, practitioners are asked to do a lot of new things. The mantra is that HR must get away from transactions, be more strategic and data driven—beyond their comfort zone. We often hear that, "it's all about the culture" and that the purpose-driven organization is authentic and delivers engagement and productivity. Robert E. Quinn and Anjan V. Thakor state in a 2018 *Harvard Business Review* article that when people pursue a higher aim, they bring with them energy and creativity. They take risks, learn, and elevate their game.[28]

> **Creating a purpose-driven organization requires attention to one's culture. Organizational culture is more about how you do something than what you do.**

In the words of Edgar Schein, culture is "the way we solve problems."[29] But be careful. Core values like integrity, empathy, trust, and transparency mean different things to different cultures and generations.

It's also about the structure!

While nurturing the organizational culture is no doubt paramount, progressive HR is also about the structure of the organization.

Organizations are bombarded with what supposedly good HR looks like in companies like Zappos, Google, and Facebook and that culture matters above all else. However, most organizations do not have the agility of the start-up mentality that can operate without cumbersome existing systems. Organizations who are not start-ups simply cannot start all over due to their legacy systems. This makes it more difficult for them to be agile. In addition, a lot of the HR functions are about (legal) compliance, grievances, background checks, record keeping, compensation management, and duty of care.

HR operates in a changing and complex context with growing regulations in all aspects of employment. Regarding the structure, in Europe we think especially about the role of the joint committees (called *paritaire commités* in Belgium and *paritaire commissies* in the Netherlands) as consultative bodies that negotiate the collective work agreements between employers and employees.

There are also increased liabilities of employers in terms of being sued by their workers, especially in the United States. Think about the #MeToo movement. While there are many calls for HR to move from "transaction to interaction," it is safe to say the administrative, structural, and legal compliance roles still must be done by HR as long as they are not (and likely cannot not be fully) automated.

#ZigZagHR-Model

Working at the strategic levels on the future of HR means that employers need to change their people value proposition (culture) and build or reengineer a new organizational architecture (structure). The return of HR value means that companies need to evolve from being an implementer and developer of policies and procedures to becoming a designer or architect of work and worker experiences.

> **Companies should find the sweet spot where the employer's expectations and the expectations of the workers meet.**

This new HR architecture is likely not a one-size-fits-all that one can buy and assemble like Ikea furniture! Innovative HR practices are not best practices that can be copied from employer to employer. Copy-paste is no longer sufficient. The new HR architecture must be flexible and able to adapt to the organization of today, tomorrow and the day after tomorrow. Common elements of the new HR architecture are that it is agile, responsive, personalized, simple, authentic, and transparent. A standardized, one-size-fits-all, approach does not work any more.

> **Each organization finds itself somewhere on a continuum from traditional "old school" to progressive "new school" and must be strategic enough to *#ZigZag* between both extremes as the context demands.**

#ZigZagHR is about what organizations need to do on the people management side to add value and remain relevant, while at the same time take into account that—unless they are a start-up organization—they cannot completely engage in tabula rasa and obliterate the full HR legacy of the past.

#ZigZagHR is not just about adding more competencies to the HR container and getting better at what we do in HR. It's about a real transformation and building an HR architecture that corresponds to the way organizations experience the people function and understand their HR role.

#ZigZagging is necessary because for most organizations, the HR legacy does not allow them to start with a clean state as if there was nothing before. There are also many stakeholder relationships that need to be managed. Think about the multiple

customers of HR: employees, labor unions, management, government, and the strict legal environment. All these relationships and customer requirements must continue to be honored and managed, while the legal and cultural context in which organizations operate prevents them from having true 'blue ocean' strategic thinking (with a wink to W. Chan Kim and Renée Mauborgne.)[30]

Change does not happen in a straight line. However, HR must innovate and respond to the possible disruption before it is too late. We have to #ZigZag because HR is in a quagmire due to a paradoxical dilemma—there are some HR functions we must continue to assume so we remain compliant with the legal and contractual context in which we operate. Other activities in our dominant HR thinking need to be abandoned and replaced with data-driven and experiential people-focused innovative solutions.

#ZigZagHR means that we adopt more progressive and innovative HR practices while holding on to some necessary traditional ones. #ZigZagHR assumes that we step back, analyze and reflect on what we currently do that we should no longer be doing. By standing by the window of our HR department, we look outside, over the wall at other organizations, or even completely different industries and sectors and get new insights. We copy-paste, adapt, and color outside of the lines.

> **#We purposefully used the subtitle of this chapter to say that HR must (dare-want-may-can) color outside of the lines, because there is no other approach. HR does not always color outside of the lines because: they don't dare as they are afraid of the unknown; they don't *want* because they resist change and don't believe in the disruption; they *may* not because there is resistance from management and the C-level; they *can't* because they don't know how!**

We are convinced that #ZigZagHR can provide an answer to the challenges that keep HR awake at night. How can I reinvent HR and my organization? How do I get my employees to be more engaged and make my company an attractive place to work? We see #ZigZagHR as a catalyst for change. We move HR innovations from the realm of the extreme to the normal and institutionalize them in our organizations. This makes us reach a higher level of HR practice.

#ZigZagHR is a continuous organic experience to scan our environment—inside and outside the boundaries of our organizations—and respond in an innovative and data-driven manner to the changing context of the work we do to accomplish our business objectives. The progressive HR practices towards which we #ZigZag today, may tomorrow or the day after tomorrow become obsolete themselves.

Anchors of the *#ZigZagHR* Model

In this *#ZigZagHR*-Model (see figure 1), HR is viewed as an ecosystem with four major anchors among which organizations tend to *#ZigZag* from traditional to progressive HR practices. They are the *#ZigZagHR*-Workforce (people), *#ZigZagHR*-Careers (work trajectories), *#ZigZagHR*-Stack (competencies), and *#ZigZagHR*-Operations (activities) that we describe briefly here and will expand upon in the next four chapters.

#ZIGZAGHR-WORKFORCE

The structural context of the workforce is changing dramatically. There is an evolution in employment classifications with the gig economy contingent workforce growing rapidly as a proportion of the total workforce. Think about the freelancers, contract workers, and other external outsourced who no longer fall under the authority of the traditional employer. As the workforce is becoming increasingly a non-employee workforce, what is the role, scope, and impact of HR with this growing segment of a flexible workforce?

Workers are becoming more diverse and they demand authenticity in the workplace. The DIBS concept (Diversity, Inclusion, Belonging and Support) is coming more and more into the forefront as a necessity for organizations. The talent acquisition sourcing modalities are also evolving from sourcing, insourcing, outsourcing, and open-source talent wherever it is available.[31]

At the same time, with developments in artificial intelligence and machine learning, many of the HR transactional HR activities are likely to be taken over by algorithms. As a result, people management is likely to focus more on the experience of employees and reducing possible pain points (creating the culture, onboarding, including the authenticity of diverse intersectional workers, developing people and leaders, rewarding performance, team work and coaching) rather than the traditional HR transactional talent practices of acquisition and employee life cycle management.

#ZIGZAGHR-STACK

The new HR architecture is based on an HR stack that goes beyond traditional HR competencies. The HR body of knowledge is still essential but has become table stakes. In *The HR Value Proposition* (2005) Dave Ulrich and Wayne Brockbank[32] argue that transactional HR activities do not really add value. Instead, HR value is created from a deep understanding of external business realities and how key stakeholders both inside and outside the company define value.

FIGURE 1. The *#ZigZagHR* Model

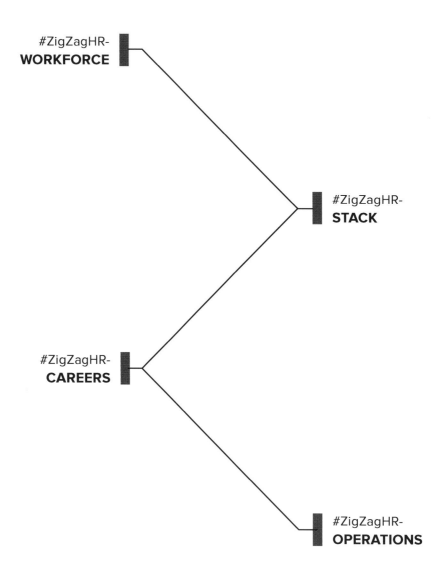

#ZigZagHR-
WORKFORCE

#ZigZagHR-
STACK

#ZigZagHR-
CAREERS

#ZigZagHR-
OPERATIONS

The traditional HR body of knowledge (HR BoK) with its functional areas is a basic competency that can be self-taught and basically learned online and/or legitimized through one of the existing HR certification processes (PHR, SPHR, GPHR, SHRM-CP, SHRM-SCP, CIPD, etc.).

The HR BoK has to be topped off with progressive HR building blocks drawn from the social sciences including design thinking (focus on employee experience touchpoints rather than HR delivery efficiency); agile management (adapt agile engineering and project management tools to HR); behavioral economics (nudge employees into making decisions that are good for them); HR analytics (use data and conduct A/B testing to drive decisions and predict behavior); and global-local savvy. Every building block has tools that can be used by HR such as: personas, user stories, scrum, social demographics, rapid prototyping, employee experience mapping, touchpoint moments of truth, behavioral nudging, sentiment analysis, data mining, cultural intelligence, etc.

#ZIGZAGHR-CAREERS

As employees are increasingly becoming a contingent workforce, many HR services are now being outsourced or delivered by freelancers. Following the rule of thumb that non-core competencies are good candidates for outsourcing, many HR transactional activities have been insourced (e.g., shared-services), outsourced (e.g., payroll, training), co-sourced with the use of a preferred vendor or consultant (e.g., duty of care), or even open-sourced (e.g., recruiting). This has resulted in having a core of very talented and strategic HR business leaders at the top (CHRO types), HR siloed specialists in the middle, and then lower-level administrative transactional shared service workers and generalists at the bottom of the HR hierarchy. This has created a middle management HR gap because the competencies of the mid-range HR practitioners are no longer sufficient to deal with the needs of the job. Most of the knowledge HR work in the middle of the HR hierarchy is project-based, data- and change management driven. This mid-range competency vacuum is currently and often filled by consultants and freelancers, people with non-HR backgrounds, or simply taken over by technology and self-service applications.

Where will progressive *#ZigZagHR* leaders ultimately come from and what is their competency profile? They will likely come equally from in- and outside of HR with a background in law, psychology, sociology, data analysis, or business management augmented with HR, project management, agile management, global savvy, experience and/or certifications.

#ZIGZAGHR-OPERATIONS

#ZigZagHR-Operations balance the day-to-day transactional HR activities with strategic partnering with the business. While using different tactics to "augment" the automation of HR transactions, progressive HR practitioners make strategic choices in each part of the operations of the enterprise.

Examples of *#ZigZagging* and dilemmas in each functional area of HR are abound: Is salary information kept confidential, or is there sunshine on pay practices through salary transparency? Are benefits motivational for employees, or is the tax structure impacting the reward value? Are the benefits geared at employees different from those of an independent contractor? Is there an accrual-based system of paid time off or is there unlimited vacation time? How can performance be paid while decoupling merit-based compensation from performance appraisals? Does the narrative of what it is like to work fit the actual employee experience? Is there generational tolerance to engage different employee segments at the level they want to be engaged? Is there reconciliation with the war on talent with the war on retention of talent? Is there an understanding of the employee sentiment (how are you feeling today towards the company?) on any given day? Are leaders of the organization attuned to the desires and expectations of employees? How concerned is the organization in developing a culture of health, safety, and security (duty of care) for workers?

With the growing application of artificial intelligence and the use of algorithms in HR management, the moral considerations surrounding these HR activities will come to the forefront. The answers to each of these questions focus on the total employee experience rather than the currently different, often siloed HR activities.

#ZigZagHR Leaders

How do you become a progressive HR workplace leader? Here are a few propositions that can serve as food for thought during the course of this book.

Progressive *#ZigZagHR* leaders:

- *Focus on the culture and the Employee Value Proposition (EVP)*—this is how you attract the best talent as an employer of choice.
- *Are customer-centric and manage the employee experience*—they deal with employee touchpoints in the pre, during, and post-employment experience as key to increase employee satisfaction, engagement, and retention of talent.
- *Recognize the different HR stakeholders and balance their often divergent requirements*—HR is too often viewed as the spokesperson for management

(and the board of directors), forgetting the interests of other important stakeholders (employees, contact workers, union, government, etc.).

- *Trust their employees*—they empower their workforce to do to the right thing with all the rights and responsibilities that trust entails.
- *Nudge their employees in the right direction*—they use behavioral nudging to make it easier for their employees to make decisions that are good for them.
- *Re-engineer the physical environment*— they create physical and virtual environments where individual and team work gets done effectively and in a wholistic manner.
- *Embrace and embed technology in HR transactions*—they augment their current transactional practices with technology to allow HR to focus on other value-added activities.
- *Integrate knowledge and tools from other management disciplines*—they know that the greatest advances in human behavior will come from the integration of knowledge and tools from other disciplines.
- *Use data to drive decisions*—they build a management culture where the basis of any decision is data driven.
- *Test prototypes*—they experiment with new practices by setting up controlled A/B testing projects and abandoning them when they fail to show results.
- *Link HR activities to the broader context*—they anticipate the constantly evolving micro, meso and macro environments of their organization and adapt (automate, abandon, reinvent) their practices accordingly.
- *Are agile*—in their ability and speed to respond to change.
- *Are both global and local*—they find the right balance between standardization and localization of their HR practices.
- *Play a key role in the societal social issues affecting their workers*—they are taking on a proactive rather than neutral role in a variety of societal issues affecting the welfare and well-being of the workforce.
- *Keep the 'H' in HR*—they make decisions focusing on the "head, heart, hand and health" of the organization as it relates to the human workforce.33

In the next chapters, we explain each of these four *#ZigZagHR* anchors in detail, provide tools to implement progressive HR practices in your organization, and show you how to become an effective *#ZigZagHR*-Leader.

IN SUMMARY

#ZigZagHR is our answer to the HR disruption brought about by the fourth industrial revolution. Our *#ZigZagHR*-Model has four anchors: *#ZigZagHR*-Workforce (people), *#ZigZagHR*-Careers (work trajectories), *#ZigZagHR*-Stack (competencies) and *#ZigZagHR*-Operations (activities). *#ZigZagHR* is about building a new and progressive culture within the structural context of our organization. We develop a few propositions to work as *#ZigZagHR*-Leaders.

3

#ZigZagHR
Workforce

THE FUTURE OF WORK:
FLEXIBILITY AND A HYBRID WORKFORCE

3

The market demands speed and agility while organizations and HR keep holding on to old systems and practices. The new reality clashes with the old HR practices! What does it mean for the people? Hold on or let go? Do the people we have on board still possess the right skill set? Hundreds, maybe thousands of people will exit the workforce or perhaps lose their jobs. In contrast, there are hundreds and thousands of openings, many that cannot be filled because people lack the required competencies. Today's context has many challenges as well as opportunities for individual workers. The way we want to live, work, and combine work and life is changing. The classic employment classification no longer fits the workplace reality and the proportion of the contingent workforce with freelance workers is growing. The classic employment status as employee is slowly but surely making room for freelancers, contract workers and other external talent that no longer necessarily passes through HR. In chapter 3, we describe how the workforce is evolving in this new reality towards a *#ZigZagHR*-Workforce, how differentiated and hybrid the workforce has become and what that means for HR. In subsequent chapters on *#ZigZagHR*-Careers and *#ZigZagHR*-Operations we dig even deeper into these issues.

In a state of Dukkha

Since the first industrial revolution, there has been an enormous trend towards hyper specialization. This manifests itself in how education is organized, how we shape our careers, how organizations are structured, and how HR attracts, develops, evaluates, and rewards talent. In 2018, we bounce against many limitations in terms of education, management practice, and HR resulting from this trend towards hyper specialization.

> **Obviously, specialization is important, but somewhere along the way hyper specialization has become the norm and clashes with what we need even more today: agility.**

Marshall Goldsmith said in a 2008 book of the same name, *What Got us Here, Won't Get Us There*.[34] There are no cookie cutter solutions in our current complex reality. The problems and challenges are becoming too complex and the context is too competitive. Currently, we are in the middle of a paradigm shift, an absolute breakpoint with the past in terms of what kind of work we do, how we work, where we work, and when we work. The changes this breakpoint engenders will have as big an impact as the first industrial revolution did centuries ago. Except, no one can really predict with a degree of certainty what the outcome will be. We know the impact will be felt globally and the speed of change will keep on increasing with as a result of a complete break with the past.

The changes in the context of work are overwhelming for many. If our environment, our worldview, and everything that we are comfortable with is constantly changing, we come into a state of *dukkha*. *Dukkha* is a Buddhist concept that describes the pain we feel when we don't know how to let go of what is no more. *Dukkha* points to a lack of satisfaction, a feeling that things no longer meet our normative expectations. And, we must all get through this...

The new workforce reality

The workforce is more mature and demands authenticity, customization, meaning, and flexibility in terms of choices with regard to where and when work is done, but also in terms of job content and rewards.

The era of one job with one employer has made room for career trajectories made up of "kaleidoscopic careers," a term Ian Sanders and David Sloly use in their book *Mash-Up* (2012), as work is increasingly done by people on a project or role basis.

> In this new *#ZigZagHR*-Reality, "generation flux" takes the lead: "multi-talented professionals who kick on complexity and constantly recalibrate."[35] We call them *#ZigZaggers*.

What is the impact of this contingent workforce? What is the relationship of HR with this flexible shell in an organization? This all makes the role of HR less clear, its impact on the organization diminished, and the nature of HR work drastically different. As a result, HR must focus its attention more on the creation of experiences for its internal (employees) and external (contract/freelance) talent. HR's attention goes towards, among other things on creating a different culture—onboarding, diversity, authenticity, development, rewards, teamwork, leadership, and coaching—rather than the traditional transactional HR practices around talent acquisition and life cycle career management.

WE LIVE LONGER, ERGO WE WORK LONGER (?)

The Belgian law, *Werkbaar en Wendbaar Werk* (Workable and Agile Work) of March 5, (2017) is the Belgian Federal Government's answer to the challenges that confronts the country in terms of employment.[36] With these decisions, the labor market should finally and definitely enter the 21st century. That's how it sounds at least. The focus of the law is to improve the working conditions during one's entire career to make it possible for people to work longer and to make the work during one's career more workable and flexible. In other words, increase work flexibility so people can remain employable longer.

Lynda Gratton and Andrew Scott argue in their book, *The 100-Year Life* that if, as predicted, one out of two people will reach 100 years of age, then the three-phased linear model of living (education, work, retirement) is no longer applicable. Instead, (work)life will be divided into multiple, shorter phases. The lockstep career, where people are rewarded solely on the basis of their function in the organization and where little consideration is given to experiences and education, is passé. Pleasant and sometimes painful transitions during one's career trajectory are becoming the norm. New work scenarios will not solely be focused on *recreation* (the promise of the leisure society), but on *re-creation* (in terms of transformation and reinvention).[37] Work and home relations will completely change. There will be more experimentation and an ongoing search for authenticity.

The era of workers spending their entire career with the same employer is (almost) over. It is also no longer evident that employees will make financial progress every year. McKinsey calculated that the salaries in the 25 richest countries increase less rapidly than the growth of the overall economy.[38] This points to a growing inequality problem. In Flanders and Belgium, this is overcome with a strong social security safety net giving

The era of workers
spending their entire career
with the same employer
is (almost) over.

the appearance that globalization creates an even greater gap between the winners and the losers. But to keep social security affordable, more people need to work and people need to work longer. This brings us back to the Belgian (Workable and Agile Work) law and the idea of guaranteed universal income that is being proposed as an alternative in many European countries.[39]

> **If we will live longer and therefore (must) work longer, it is important to constantly reinvent ourselves.**

In *Stretch, How to Futureproof Yourself for Tomorrow's Workplace*, the authors Karie Willyerd and Barbara Mistick propose a mindset and a few strategies to remain relevant today, tomorrow, and the day after tomorrow. The authors describe "stretch" as, "to reach beyond your capabilities of today to be ready for tomorrow, to expand your viewpoint and skills beyond your current state and to be relentlessly resourceful in pursuing your career dreams."[40]

On the advice of George W. Crane (1901-1995), "there is no future in any job." The future lies in the man who holds the job," we like to add that this holds today for *any man or woman*!

CAREER CHANGE IS THE NEW NORMAL
AND THE ONLY WAY IS NO LONGER UP

In the futuristic *Charlie and the Chocolate Factory* by Roald Dahl, the elevators don't go up and down. They go sideways and diagonally, and that's a great metaphor for how careers evolve today. Back in the day, career success was synonymous with a straight line up. Today, more and more people want to be challenged and develop in breadth and/or in depth, and they demand from their employers to be given the necessary space and tools to be able to develop and grow. Some people are sometimes taking a step backwards—it's called demotion—meaning they assume a lower function or role whether they are forced to or by choice. This may be coupled with a reduction in salary, privileges but also likely reduced work pressures.

> #In too many companies, the demand by workers for flexibility is still met with a one-size-fits-all approach and in a rather paternalistic manner, with an "I know what is good for you" mentality. There are not many futuristic elevators in most organizations, meaning that workers are feeling trapped in boxes, job descriptions and pre-determined career paths.

In his LinkedIn blog (March 8, 2018), Gustavo Razetti pleads for a different form of career development and that employers must shift from a "job-focused to a people-centered career planning."[41]

PIVOT OR PERSEVERE – ZOOMING IN & ZOOMING OUT

Everyone experiences a "pivot or persevere" hinge moment during one's career: the moment when one must make a choice to take another road or stay with the same employer. Pivot and persevere are terms derived from the "lean start-up" methodology of Eric Ries and refer to the moment when an entrepreneur must decide whether to further develop an initial idea (persevere) or to take another direction (pivot). During one such "pivot or persevere" moment, it is important to be able to zoom in or out. Even when there is no concrete hinge moment, it is good to regularly take distance and look for possibly different perspectives.[42]

> **Just like products, professionals also have a "sell-by date". In order not to become obsolete, professionals are better off when they disrupt themselves before realizing one day their skill set is no longer relevant.**

WORK-LIFE INTEGRATION RATHER THAN WORK-LIFE BALANCE

As Dolly Parton sings, "Working 9 to 5, what a way to make a living," work-life balance is at the top of the agenda today. We have been talking about this in HR for many years already! When we say work-life balance, we mean that one is capable of dividing one's day in obligations that relate to work as well as those that deal with one's private life. In the past, work was not taken home and home was separated from work. Clear (?). Not anymore! Now the separation between work and life is fading. The idea of work-life balance is being replaced by work-life integration as a better and more realistic alternative for ambitious professionals who find both their work and private life equally important and are looking for a way to develop both simultaneously.[43]

Thanks to technological and communications developments, we are able to work where we want and when we want, and even more: it is becoming the norm. This means that during the workday, professionals are taking on other tasks (shopping, picking up kids from school, attending events, and eating together) and in return, often continue work when the kids are in bed or after having dinner with friends.

When implementing work-life integration policies, it is crucial to clarify what is acceptable so that the advantages of one employee do not negatively impact another. Communication of clear expectations is a priority, as well as setting boundaries for employees who don't work enough or work too much.

The illiterate of the 21st Century will not be those who cannot read and write, but those who cannot learn, unlearn, and relearn.

Alvin Toffler

LEARNING A LIVING: LEARN – UNLEARN – RELEARN

As Alvin Toffler said, "the illiterate of the 21st Century will not be those who cannot read and write, but those who cannot learn, unlearn and relearn."

To survive "The Future of Work" people must constantly learn, which is not limited to going back to school or take training courses. It also means "learning on the fly" as described in *Stretch, How to Futureproof Yourself* by Karie Willyerd en Barbara Mistick.[44] "Learning on the fly" refers to the degree to which one is willing and able to learn from day-to-day situations as a result of a having a growth-mindset through: an extreme measure of curiosity and inquisitiveness; by building in time to reflect; by observing and knowing when to abandon old assumptions; and by letting go of obsolete knowledge.

Organizations and managers can stimulate their workforce to learn from each other by giving them the freedom, space, time, and means to learn. A learning culture can take on different forms. Think, for example on providing free access to easily available information and content via social media, TedX, Coursera, Udacity, the Khan Academy, and others. Companies can also organize a "playground" during lunch time or end-of-the workweek "learning arenas"where workers share their knowledge with each other, supported or not by an app or digital platform.

Informal learning and knowledge sharing can also be stimulated by organizing the work space, such as coffee areas, sitting areas, and even ping pong tables. Following the example of Sweden, worldwide organizations who (at a minimum) have a daily *fika* moment: a cup of coffee with a cinnamon roll (or energy bar). The term fika dates from the 19th century and is the vernacular for *kaffi*, the Swedish word for coffee in those days. But today, *fika* means more than a quick chat at the coffee machine. At 11am workers in Sweden interrupt work for a joint *fika*. Nobody stays at their desk in the office and it becomes an ideal opportunity to socialize with one's colleagues. Afterwards, they continue work with increased concentration.

By promoting internal talent mobility, employees who desire to learn can take on other roles faster and sustain their employability. Internal mobility—or the switching of functions by employees within the organization—can take different directions and does not always need to be an upward move. In each direction, the employee will be challenged and learn. Less common in Belgium is perhaps the mid-life internship that is not limited to students. Think about the movie *The Intern*, the story of seventy-year old Ben (played Robert De Niro) who is bored to death as a recent retiree. Under the guise of "gray is the new green," he gets an internship at a successful online fashion company and, in the shortest of times, he makes himself indispensable. Not only does the company win (tacit knowledge and experience!), but also the "gray intern" who has a hard time getting a job, although he financially may not need to work as hard, makes himself meritorious.

By implementing a job rotation program—a push-through system where employees on a team or in a department regularly change jobs—employees can learn new functions and task packages and keep on learning.

For decades, Belgium has tried at the societal level to introduce life-long learning as a must for reschooling. But, it failed as the shoe pinched at all levels—the employee, the job hunter and the employer.

> **Learning is still being viewed too much as an expense rather than an investment. A term like life-long earning likely does not help either as it gives the impression of a punishment rather than an opportunity. Learning is still viewed as a pill that must be taken to get better.**

In Germany, life-long learning is called *Bildung* (building—as in body building) and has a much broader connotation. *Bildung* refers to personal development and growth.

According to Douglas Thomas and John Seely Brown, the half life of a skill today is barely five years. That means what you learned 10 years ago is now obsolete and that half of what you learned five years ago is already irrelevant today. As a result, our careers are shapeshifting and every four and a half or five years we (must) change jobs. In their book, *A New Culture of Learning*, they plead for a new method of education, learning, and training.[45] Since the shelf-life of our knowledge has an always shortening half-life, our universities must, in their teaching/educating focus more and more on critical thinking and life-long learning skills such as creativity, problem solving, critical analysis, leadership, teamwork, curiosity, experimentation, and experiential learning rather than the acquisition of explicit knowledge. Experiential learning or "learning by doing" is a process where knowledge, skills, abilities, and attitudes are acquired inductively by practice rather than by solely learning the theory.

OVERWHELMED AND DISENGAGED VERSUS MAVERICKS AND NEO-GENERALISTS

We expect people to be always on today, to be the drivers of their own careers, to continuously learn and keep up, because many jobs will be taken over by computers and algorithms. In the meantime, management pushes the pressure down from the top to the bottom. No wonder that employee engagement has never been as low and the number of people who mentally and physically check out has never been as high.[46]

Not everyone can deal with this new reality. On the one end of the workforce continuum, there are people who fall out, who can no longer keep up. They are not capable of reinventing themselves and miss the resilience to pursue—whether forced or not—a career change and give new direction to their professional life.

On the other end of the continuum are the mavericks, the learnatics, the neo-generalists who surf on the wave of change. The term maverick refers to an independently thinking person, a misfit, who does not conform. "Learnatic" is a term introduced by Sebastian Bailey, co-founder of Mindgym.[47] According to him, organizations must hire learnatics, or professionals with a strong urge for freedom, flexibility and autonomy and an insatiable hunger for learning. These often experienced professionals dare say goodbye to the golden cage. They don't stubbornly hold on to the classical linear career, but pivot effortlessly from one role to the next, where the challenge and content of the work primes over status. Enter the "hybrid" career, or #ZigZag-Careers as we like to call them.

BLENDED KNOWLEDGE, BEYOND THE BOUNDARIES OF TRADITIONAL DISCIPLINES

"Labels stick, only if we let them!" This is a quote from the *The Neo-Generalist*, a book by Kenneth Mikkelsen and Richard Martin.[48] A neo-generalist is, at the same time, a specialist and a generalist who is capable of shifting to another niche as the context requires.

Neo-generalists are the bridge builders between different specialisms, they innovate where others can't by mixing expertise and ideas from totally divergent domains.

Mikkelsen and Martin call this "dragonfly vision", referring to the composite multifaceted eyes of the dragonfly. Their book is a plea for an inter- and multi-disciplinary approach. According to Mikkelsen and Martin, the neo-generalists possesses the meta skills that the 2020 workforce will need. Some of those meta skills are to be able to connect the dots; able to make connections and see the larger picture; skills that must be engaged to address complex challenges.

Neo-generalists are able to bridge and bond. Bonding is connecting people with the same convictions and bridging is connecting people with a totally different worldview. Neo-generalists purposefully seek out people with another worldview. Neo-generalists collect and integrate knowledge from different disciplines and make something new out of it: copy-adapt-paste instead of copy-paste because the latter no longer works. By taking ideas from one discipline and applying it to another one, true transformation is possible. As a result, neo-generalists move things and people and even entire organizations.

The new composite "hybrid" workforce

The classic employment status no longer corresponds with the new reality as the proportion of the contingent workforce with flexible workers is increasing. More and more, we speak about the gig-economy and the NextGen Work.

The terms contingent workforce is a collective name for anyone who, by definition, is hired temporarily to take on a specific task; who is paid on the basis of the total number of hours effectively worked; and does not enjoy the benefits, protection, and secondary working conditions that an employee on the payroll usually has.

The gig economy, also sometimes called freedom or platform economy, originated as a sort of by-product of the on-demand economy, an economy where people do not work in a fixed employment status, but rather in short-term paid gigs.

NextGen Work is a collective noun for all possible forms of contracts where professionals can step in: interim, freelance, independent, platformworker, and slasher. Slasher stands for a one person/multiple careers and professionals who take on different and divergent roles, often as freelancers.

FROM COLLECTIVE STANDARD TO INDIVIDUAL CUSTOMIZED WORK

Anno 2018, the economy is working at full speed. The scarcity of talent has mainly become structural, job openings are not being filled, and the nature of work is constantly changing. Employers are continuously looking for new competencies and are counting more and more on flexible solutions. Hence, the flexible contract workforce is increasing vis-à-vis the core of employees.

A core of fixed employees still remains very important for the efficient and effective execution of the core business of an organization while the flexible workforce can temporarily be deployed to respond in a viable manner to the uncertainty of the supply and demand of talent in a rapidly changing context.

Yet, such a flexible workforce is no guarantee for success. Employers must strategically manage their make-versus-buy talent choices (see further the notion of Total Talent Management). In addition, this new reality of a shrinking core workforce and increasing contingent workforce also has an impact on the DNA and culture of the organization.

Where a good employer for our (grand)parents provided stability and security, a good employer in The Future of Work is someone who cares about the people who work for them, get stronger in their growth and development, and encourages them to move, even beyond the boundaries of their own firm.

> **An employer is no longer the boss, but a partner in the talent development of a team of collaborators. A successful employee is no longer an individual with knowledge, skills, and abilities, but someone who can use their competencies in connection with the team and work in an agile environment.**

EMPLOYEES AND INDEFINITE CONTRACTS: OVER AND OUT?

In the United States, the legal relations between an employer and employee (outside of labor contracts negotiated with the unions) is generally "at-will employment." This means both the employer and the employee can end the working relationship in a short period of time (usually two weeks). But the principle of contract employment of a particular duration—and without the same compensation and benefits—has been increasing enormously over the past few years. Employees and contract workers with different employment status often work side-by-side in the same jobs which can create inequalities in their status.

Although the classical Belgian employment contract of indefinite duration is not disappearing, the evolution towards "workers of a thousand shades," an image used by the professional journal *HR Square* in its fall 2017 conference, can no longer be denied. There are many flexible solutions in addition to the fixed contract of (in) definite duration: temporary agency work is a motor for and barometer of flexibility, part-time work, student internships, and the flexible workforce of people who are not employees. Expressed in annual numbers, for every 1000 employees with a contract of indefinite duration in Belgium, there are 104 with a contract of finite duration, 77 temp workers, 89 interns, 45 freelancers, 56 project workers, and 51 people on temporary unemployment benefits.[49]

Project workers, temporary workers, detached workers, freelancers, independent entrepreneurs, and employer groups are different employment statutes and structures that show how employers are searching for creative solutions to quickly acquire flexible expertise. Employer groups use a system where they unite to employ and share workers collectively to fill their talent needs. In other words, several organizations jointly hire workers to put them to work simultaneously or successively. Following the French example, employer groups were experimentally included in the Belgian employment law of 2014 and renewed annually. After the 2014 relaxation of the employment law, the social partners negotiated without results over the flexible employment modalities.

The new 2017 law on Workable and Agile Work made flexible work a definite system, simplified and extended it. This concretely means an employer group can hire workers and make them available (i.e., subcontract them) for its members. With regard to the worker, the only employer is the employer group.[50] The system of employer groups offers many opportunities especially for small enterprises who don't have the means to hire (extra) workers full time. In spite of the benefits and relaxation of the new law, its success is still very limited, which makes examples scarce. In 2016, the first employer group was introduced in Flanders. The administrative wheels had to turn for at least one year before a chocolate factory in Bruges could employ flexible workers. The owner of the chocolate factory also operated a tearoom. Although both establishments were right across from each other, employees from the chocolate factory, who were only busy during peak periods of the year, could not help during their slack time in the tearoom that was busy all year around.

Co-sourcing is another example of flexible work. In co-sourcing, talent crosses the boundaries of the organization and is shared with another employer. A win for the lending employer (experienced workers can remain employed and part of the employment costs are recuperated), and for the borrowing employer (a senior profile is provided at the cost of a junior without passively accruing social costs), for the worker (who can deploy expert talent and grow) and for society (burn-out is reduced and people stay employed longer). Co-sourcing can be considered as a multi-company career center.

THE BARK IS WORSE THAN THE BITE...
In Belgium, the majority of workers still prefer the classic employment contract of indefinite duration. The labor unions also show their explicit preference for a fixed employment contract. In Europe as a whole, fixed employment contracts represent only 58% percent. In Belgium, that number is considerably higher.[51] In the U.S., it is predicted that in the next decades, contract work will represent the majority of the American workforce. This already holds true for millennials who are 50% freelancers (although often as a second job). The growth of the American freelance workforce is three times faster than the growth of the traditional workforce.[52]

FLEX IS HERE TO STAY!

While Belgium, compared to the rest of Europe and the U.S., keeps hanging onto a traditional workforce, the advance of external talent is growing quickly. The five major reasons for using external talent are:

- Acquiring the right expertise
- Filling jobs temporarily
- Supplementing the workforce during peak seasons
- Quickly getting professional help
- Organizational transformation and change

Depending on the maturity phase and professionalization, the use of external talent is often decentralized. Recruitment is coordinated in consultation with multiple departments, often through a Preferred Supplier List (PSL). A central region optimizes the entire process, whether or not with a Master Vendor (MV). In the best of case, this process is an integral component of the entire HR sourcing and talent strategy called Total Talent Acquisition (TTA).

Let's zoom in on freelancing, because it manifests itself undoubtedly as one of the important emerging forms of work in the labor market and one of the new business models.

FREELANCING: SHAPING THEIR OWN WORK AND LIVES

The number of freelancers in Flanders is estimated at 120,000 although no official numbers are available. This corresponds to five to seven freelancers per 100 workers, four to five in primary employment, and one to two in secondary employment.[53] It is only an estimate as there is no separate legal status for freelancers. The statistics are hard to distinguish between employees and other workers, and the "freelancer" concept is ill defined. It is a contemporary form of work that is not linked to a specific sector and can entail many different functions and jobs done by the freelancer based on expertise, work creativity, and accomplishments with greater autonomy in terms of organization of work. According to the *Stichting Innovatie & Arbeid* (Foundation for Innovation & Work), a freelancer is an independent who has no employees and "leases" one's work, knowledge, and creativity to organizations. That often happens on a project basis.[54] With 1.3 million, the Netherlands counts the highest proportion of freelancers in the workforce in Europe. In the rest of Europe, the freelance phenomenon is growing as well.[55]

The McKinsey report entitled *Independent Work in the Gig-Economy*, published in the fall of 2016, illustrated the phenomenon of the independent workforce in Europe and the U.S.[56] This report also highlights that more and more people choose to take their life and career in their own hands and opt for an independent contractor status. But even here, few statistics are given because "the freelancer" does not really exist as an employment category.

The emergence of freelancers fits in the broader trend where the proportion of "standard work" (the fulltime employee) decreases and the proportion of "non-standard work" (self-employed, part-time or full-time partial work, permanent part-time work) increases. The plug-and-play character of freelancers, the specific expertise, and the cost structure explain broadly why more and more companies use freelancers. The advance of non-standard types of work is likely irreversible and comes as any change with the necessary challenges. The freedom of a freelance career goes hand in hand with a large amount of uncertainty. This development calls for new political questions. Is this a trend that should be encouraged by society? What should we let go and what should we regulate? What place do freelancers have in the social, fiscal, and legal system?

In Belgium, there is a gap with the legal employment framework and the rise of freelancers. There are great differences and work-related benefits between the independent contractor and the fixed salaried employee in working for the same employer: differences regarding the specificity of the social status of independent workers with different regulations related to costs and taxes, social security contributions, guaranteed income, healthcare benefits, worker's compensation, work accidents, occupational illnesses, vacations, paternal leave, time credits, other thematic leave of absences, unemployment, and pension accruals. In addition, there are also differences in terms of work security, working times, legal protection, right to representation, collective bargaining, and other working rights related to non-discrimination and worker-subsidized training and development. While the need and interest of employers to use flexible and agile talent increases, the government has not yet figured out how to manage this.[57]

FREELANCERS: CANARY, CHICKEN, OR CUCKOO CHICK?
For some, freelancers are the "canaries in the coal mine"—an unmistakeable signal that something is drastically changing in the labor market. Others compare the rise of the freelancers as a "cuckoo chick" and see this trend as a dishonest competition between independent contractors and employees, where the latter gets the worst of it. And for others still, freelancers are "the chicken with the golden egg"—an important source of flexibility and new entrepreneurship.

Employees often feel disadvantaged and say "the freelancers get the fun projects and we have to keep doing the boring routine work." Employers need to switch fast and need the competencies and expertise they do not (yet) have in-house. So, they call in external

The proportion of "standard work" decreases while the proportion of "non-standard work" increases.

contingent workers. Perhaps, they do have this expertise somewhere in house, but it is simply not visible because of existing silos. Perhaps, HR must focus on both: career management to further develop internal expertise and talent mobility AND the use external expertise.

Impact on HR

The growth of the non-traditional workforce has a number of consequences for HR, not only regarding the legal status or classification of workers, but also for cooperation, compensation and benefits.

WHAT IS THE CORRECT WORKER CLASSIFICATION?

Terms of employment apply to all workers and require compliance. However, the fast growth of the non-traditional workforce has created a gap between the new reality and the existing administrative and socio-legal framework. A big challenge for HR is to correctly classify workers. Are they employees or independent contractors? Or perhaps, the worker is a pretend independent contract? How much autonomy does the worker have over the job tasks? How much control does the employer or third-party have over the worker? When there is a conflict or law suit, it is quite uncertain which way the verdict will go. How is the employment relationship interpreted? Are Uber drivers or Deliveroo couriers, for example, employees or independent contractors?

OPERATING WITH A BLENDED WORKFORCE

Tasks that are done by a freelancer shifts the control over work and tools to that worker. This is also one of the decisive arguments to legally classify a freelancer as an independent worker. This shift requires a different management approach (whether it concerns a project or a process) where there is no question of direct control over the freelancer and the tasks that are executed.

In addition, professionals with different employment statuses work side-by-side in teams on common projects. Managing such hybrid teams requires different management and leadership competencies that go beyond the traditional management-employee relationship.

#To stimulate the performance of people—whether internal or external talent—HR must work closely with the business and ensure that management has the appropriate leadership competencies to lead and motivate blended teams.

Leena Nair, the first female and also youngest CHRO ever at Unilever, talks in that context about the "inner game" and the "outer game" in leadership. The "outer game" is all about business acumen and a catalyst for talent, while the" inner game" is about learning agility, self management, and resilience (soft skills). Today, too little attention is directed towards the attraction and development of leaders. According to her, the importance of the "inner game" is increasing in leadership.[58]

> # An additional challenge for HR is supporting remote workers so these workers are socialized in the same organizational culture and have a sense of belonging. More importantly, HR must find a way to ensure these remote workers know they are supported.

ADEQUATE COMPENSATION AND BENEFITS

One of the disadvantages of working as a freelancer is undoubtedly not enjoying most employee benefits—both short term as well as long term. Although we presume that millennials would favor short-term rewards and a flexible lifestyle, they will inevitably as they age and have greater interest in building a nest egg. Preferences and opinions differ widely from country to country. In addition, no single generation has ever saved as much in their young age as millennials in spite of many carrying heavy student loans for the years to come.[59] The American younger generation is uncertain about their future and worry that the rise of artificial intelligence, that people live longer and must work longer, that temporary and on-demand work is increasing—and all of that without a social safety net. In Belgium, where there is a mature and extensive social safety net, the call to work longer is met with demonstrations and other forms of protest. A list of what are considered "heavy occupations" may expedite the retirement age for some. A big and diverse group, from teachers to construction workers, would qualify for early (earlier) retirement. As we write this book, there is still no clarity as to which jobs fall under these "heavy occupations" or not.

In pay for performance, employers generally pay employees (=salary) for their competencies and reward them (=bonus) for their contributions. Another challenge for HR consists of engaging and motivating a blended workforce. Work is less and less being paid for through standard compensation. Compensation and benefits will need to be customized to meet the different needs of different workers—whether on the payroll or not.

Customization of rewards is a difficult thing because very different career trajectories exist within the same organization, which can have negative consequences. Some employers have come up with tons of creative solutions for customization of benefits such as: paying off student loans; nudging people to save for retirement; providing extra services to help families combine family and work better; from ironing (yes still somewhat important in Belgium) to shopping and childcare; flexibility regarding where, when, and how to work, etc. With these benefits, they want to accommodate the wishes and needs at the individual contributor level and satisfy both the traditional as well as non-traditional workforce.

Ultimately, talent is talent

The time has come for HR to take charge of the recruitment and selection of external (in addition to internal) talent and develop a strategic vision around workforce staffing options. One of the big challenges will be to navigating the legal ambiguities and distinguishing the trees from the forest. Employees pass through HR, freelancers not necessarily. They are often flying under the radar (called stealth workers). Therefore, HR often does not have the exact picture of the total full-time equivalent and the associated labor costs. And what about work environment, culture, communication, and engagement? It is crucial that HR takes full responsibility for the total workforce. Otherwise, the attraction of the external (contract) workforce becomes a game of cheaper labor, and solely focusing on labor cost is rarely the most sustainable solution.

We are evolving towards a tri-partite situation where the direct relationship between employer and employee is making room for intermediaries: a temporary employment agency, an interim-management agency, a platform.

Total talent management: A marriage between HR and purchasing?

Worldwide, we can expect the difference between the fixed and flexible workforce planning—in terms of HR processes and activities—will decrease and, in the near future, both categories of workers will be searched for through the same talent acquisition channels and processes.

> Instead of focusing on fixed recruitment functions, the HR roles, tasks, and responsibilities of finding the optimal workforce can be better delineated. This is one of the basic principles of *Total Talent Management* (TTM) or *Total Talent Acquisition* (TTA).

It is high time that HR gets involved in the recruitment and selection of external contract talent while developing a strategic vision around contract workers.

TTM and TTA are more than just finding the right candidates. Because the needs and the supply of talent are continuously evolving, this impacts the role of HR as a purchaser of talent. Currently, TTA is generally the domain of purchasing and not really HR. Purchasing tends to be very familiar with this "contract labor" approach, because it is common for them to develop business and financial plans and justify these investments to management. HR will need to invoke the influx of the externs to attract the necessary competencies that an organization needs (TTA) and engage the talent towards the strategic needs of the organization (TTM). A stronger working relationship between HR and Purchasing will help them to be successful in a competitive market.

THINK LIKE A MARKETER

Luk Smeyers, CEO and co-founder of iNostix at Deloitte, used the phrase "listening data" in one of his monthly HR Square columns (January 2018).[60] Because the context in which people work today has fundamentally changed, HR must urgently start thinking and acting from the perspective of the end customer, similarly to what marketing has been doing. This applies to every team worker and not exclusively HR. Marketers permanently listen to (potential) clients and that "listening data" couples the smart marketers to the results of their campaigns. However, HR does not really listen and instead of customizing relevant microsegments, HR divides employees up in into categories such as departments, job titles, or functions which may no longer be relevant to the business. Perhaps it is better to use psychographics segmentation on the workforce, such as lifestyles, interests, worldviews, and beliefs.

IN SUMMARY

The new work reality has important consequences for individual workers and employers. Working longer, making transitions to constantly reinvent oneself, life-long learning, and the need to integrate work and life all have an enormous impact on engagement and well-being of the worker. The social contract between the employer and the employee is eroding and evolving. We see a clear trend towards the growth of freelance professionals both in absolute and relative numbers. This has advantages and disadvantages, so HR must take a new approach to talent acquisition and management.

4

#ZigZagHR
Stack

A NEW SKILLSET BEYOND HR

4

The changes that we described in chapter 1 (demography, technology, and globalization) not only impacted work, but also the workers who are also disrupting HR. Progressive companies see that traditional HR practices such as recruitment, selection, and performance management (to name a few) no longer meet what candidates and workers expect from HR. Now that the focus is on creating meaningful employee experiences, HR is consciously saying goodbye to old (traditional) HR practices, policies, and procedures that no longer offer added value. Instead, they muster new practices (especially) outside of HR from other management disciplines: design thinking, agile management, behavioral economics, analytics, and considerations between global standarization and local responsiveness. While this approach is promising, sustainable change will only result in productivity and engagement gains if we can revive the H in HR.

Is current HR still relevant?

With these transformations in the world of work and the worker, it is easy to fall behind. Continuing to work the way we do in HR will no longer be sufficient as we will not only fall behind, but miss the next opportunity and become irrelevant. We cannot survive or be relevant with our current practices that are based on a fixed mindset or things we are stuck on because we have always been doing it that way. Instead, we must adopt a flexible mindset and continue to learn, adapt, and experiment with new approaches. Yet, this does not mean we need to embrace every new HR fad and copy it within our workplace. On the contrary, we must make strategic choices, customize new concepts to our company, implement new ways so they make sense to our workforce, and find ways to measure whether we are able to achieve the intended objective.

> **To replace the current (read: obsolete) paradigm with a fundamentally new talent management vision, HR must borrow from other management disciplines.**

Today's progressive HR practitioner must augment traditional HR knowledge and functions with skills and tools from other disciplines. In essence, HR must do what is called "stack" in IT—manage people and processes across an organization using a collection of external and internal tools, technologies, and solutions.[61]

The new *#ZigZagHR*–Stack is made up of:

- Design thinking (strategy)
- Behavioral economics (where psychology and economics meet)
- Agile management (project management)
- Analytics (data analysis and management sciences)

These four building blocks are part of a new and more progressive HR architecture that offers a new future for HR.

Design thinking

The origin of design thinking dates back to 1950s with the development of creativity techniques and new design methods in the 1960s. L. Bruce Archer was the first author to use the terms "design thinking" in his book *Systematic Methods for Designers* (1965).[62] Design thinking is an alternative to classical linear processes and is based on creativity, logic, intuition, and data as evidence. Simply stated, it is a way of thinking and working to solve complex problems in a practical and creative manner and to develop (read: design) new products and services. As a result, it is often used in innovation.

> **Design thinking always starts from the (needs of the) client who is then also involved in the co-creation.**

Design thinking is an iterative process where multi-disciplinary teams work together. A design thinking process usually—according to the source consulted—consists of (four to six) different phases:[63]

1. Empathize (understand)
2. Observe (listen)
3. Define (define the problem)
4. Ideate (generate ideas)
5. Prototype (develop a prototype)
6. Test (test the proposed solution)

Concretely, design thinking can be used for most HR-related challenges that matter to companies such as increasing retention, decreasing burn out and absenteeism, fostering a new organizational culture, and redesigning HR processes. It can also help design innovative solutions that improve the employee experience as consumers of HR products, services, and processes along the employee life cycle.

By applying design thinking, HR gets a more realistic picture of the specific challenges from the perspective of employees by mapping the employee experience including all interactions (touchpoint management) with HR and the organization.[64] This allows HR to redefine the challenges employees encounter—not from the perspective of HR but from the point of view of employees—and design creative and workable solutions based on feedback and data (rapid prototyping). The power of rapid prototyping is that, very quickly, many possible solutions are generated that are simple to implement. The simplicity and speed of this model can help HR improve the employee experience and the various touchpoints rather than focusing on the HR process itself.

In other words, in design-centric culture, HR gets to understand and improve the employee's emotional experience with the organization. In design thinking, three core principles apply:

- **EMPATHY**: HR understands the problems employees face.
- **IMAGINATION**: HR proposes creative solutions to improve the employee experience.
- **EXPERIMENTATION**: HR tests, improves, and optimizes the solution with feedback and data.[65]

There are different tools for each phase in the design thinking process. We zoom in on a few: namely employee experience mapping, touchpoint management, and rapid prototyping.

EMPLOYEE EXPERIENCE MAPPING

"How to win the war for talent by giving employees the workspaces they want, the tools they need and a culture to celebrate." This is the theme of *The Employee Experience Advantage* by Jacob Morgan. He looks at three factors (the physical environment, technology, and organizational culture) that have a positive or negative impact on how employees interact with HR and experience the organization.[66]

First, "the physical environment" has an undeniable impact on the employee experience. According to Jacob Morgan, the ideal physical environment is COOL with LinkedIn, Google, Zappos, and AirBnB as examples. COOL is an acronym for:

- **C**hooses to bring in friends or visitors
- **O**ffers flexibility
- **O**rganization's values are affected
- **L**everages multiple workspace options

This is what COOL looks like:

- The employer stimulates its employees by allowing them to bring their family and friends to visit them at work (at Facebook, four friends can hang out at the workplace, while Amazon has a bring-your-parent-to-work day).
- The employer gives employees the flexibility to partially work at home or wherever they want so that life and work can be better integrated.
- The design of the workplace corresponds to the values of the organization.
- The employer has several workspace modalities. This is more than the endless discussions about landscaping the office environment and it does not mean

that our physical workplaces all need to look like a Google campus. At Ikea, employees can, for example, decorate their own office...with Ikea furniture of course! At AirBnB, employees have a budget to give their workplace a unique look based on their own preferences.

Second, "technology" also impacts how employees experience their work environment. By technology we mean hardware, software, user interface design, HR software, apps and much more. Many employees are frustrated over the lack of tools or having to work with old or defective tools. Even if they find their job challenging and have a good relationship with their manager and co-workers, they would still change jobs out of frustration with the existing tools and technology. This is because today, technology is embedded in everything they do at work, including communication and cooperation. So, if the tools are not functioning, communication and cooperation suffer.

Third, there is the "culture" that defines how employees experience their company and HR. Compared to the physical environment and technology, culture is not tangible. However, how others perceive the organization; the degree to which everyone feels appreciated in the workplace and can be fully engaged; and the importance the company puts on well being at work all can have an enormous impact on how employees experience their employer. Imagine that you are super excited to start a new job with a company (there seems to be a 100% fit), but your friends don't think the company is a great place to work. For sure, this will have an impact on how you experience your first day at work and how long you may want to stay with them.

Employee experience mapping, also called employee journey mapping, compares the employee experience with the customer journey in marketing. It charts the complete experience an employee has when interacting (touchpoints) with your organization. The entire life cycle as an employee is mapped before, during and after their journey.[67] There are several best practices in terms of how to build an experience map and, more specifically, an employee journey map.[68]

Applying the marketing principles of a customer experience to the HR employee experience requires the segmentation of employees and the creation of different personas based on the drivers and desires of employees. Then, the employee journey is mapped according to all the contacts or touchpoints they have when engaging with HR and the company during the complete work or employee life cycle.

We recommend that experience mapping should be done for everyone who works in the organization including candidates, employees, contingent workers and even alumni of the employer and also to extend this practice to part-time workers and external talent. In that regard, it is probably better in mapping to use the terms "workforce experience" and "workforce journey" rather than employee experience and employee journey.[69]

The development of the employee experience map requires both qualitative and quantitative data. The qualitative insights for the employee experience map are usually collected through in-depth interviews with employees representing different personas. The quantitative data come from ambient data that is owned by the organization on employees and employee self- reported data through engagement or pulse surveys. These user stories are then written up in a more structured manner using a "doing, thinking, feeling" framework. What is it that people are doing?—their behavior—how are people feeling about this?—their emotions—and what are they thinking?—their assumptions and rationale.[70]

In questioning people, we may want to ask the following: which part of your job gives you the greatest energy? What is the best aspect of our organizational culture? Which competencies do you use the most in the work you currently do? Where do you get the information to do your job well? Why did you come to work here? However, what you hear must be supplemented with what you observe in the behavior of your employees, the word they use (or don't use), how they feel, and what brings them fear and anxiety.

TOUCHPOINT MANAGEMENT

Employees have different interactions (touchpoints) with HR during their life cycle with their employer. Touchpoints are the emotional points of contact the employee has with the organization as an internal customer—whether through structures, systems or people.

Once an employee experience map has been designed, it is critical for the HR team to develop an inventory of all the touchpoints the employee has with the processes, products and services that HR provides and through which channel (virtual or f2f) these touchpoints are experienced.[71]

A few examples illustrate the importance of managing HR touchpoints:

- How do new applicants perceive their contacts with you as an employer—when they are invited for an interview, whether they get hired or rejected as an applicant, during their first day at work, or after a long period of absence?
- How do remote workers get support and coaching from their managers when they have limited face-to-face interactions?
- How easy is it for employees to navigate the self-service HR portal?
- What opportunities for development and growth do employees have in your organization?
- How well are they supported and coached by their managers?

Each touchpoint can be experienced either positively by employees (a great experience) or are viewed negatively (pain points). HR must provide a seamless set of services that enable work productivity and improve the overall employee experience and must handle all the touchpoints with people (managers, HR and co-workers), tools, systems, policies and procedures—from the employee's point of view rather than the HR process and delivery perspective.

Note that the employee experience is not necessarily uniform for each employee as one segment or group of employees is likely to experience the various touchpoints with HR somewhat differently. Therefore, it is good to identify different customer personas.

A persona is an ideal type of a typical employee who is representative of a group of people with similar behavioral characteristics, needs, and experiences. In the same way that marketing segments its customers with personas to better understand potential customer, so too can personas be used to better understand employees and approach them more effectively in a customized manner. For example, an older worker has different wants and needs and, therefore, may experience the benefit policies in a totally different manner than a millennial worker. The global standard that you have for certain HR practices (i.e., non-smoking or alcohol consumption rules) is likely experienced differently in various geographies where you operate. The labeling of the employment status according to different people working on the same team (employee vs. freelance) is likely going to affect their sense of belonging and work experience. The greater flexibility afforded to some employees (usually based on their rank or status) is likely experienced differently from the worker who has limited or no opportunity for flexibility.

Hence, employee experience mapping is not a one-size-fits-all proposition. It has to be customized for each persona (demographics, job function, work location, etc.). Thus, it is necessary to use the lens or overriding filter through which a particular persona views the employee journey. Multiple maps must eventually be developed based on the wants and needs of the segmented employee persona groups.[72]

Developing employee experience maps allows HR to gain insight into what their employees are doing, thinking, and feeling rather than looking at HR practices from the perspective of the provision of HR services. It allows HR to acquire a more empathetic understanding of how employees experience the touchpoints with the HR organization and how to improve them, if needed, by focusing their HR budgets, time, and resources on improving or redesigning these interactions. This helps HR to better conceptualize what it means to belong to the organization, measure various aspects of belonging, and implement a culture where everyone belongs, albeit in different ways.

RAPID PROTOTYPING

Design thinking uses prototypes to explore possible solutions.[73] Rapid prototyping is a collective noun for different techniques that make it possible to quickly develop prototypes. Call it a form of experimentation, where a preliminary rough original model—representing the embodiment of an idea—is built quickly to allow questions to be asked and choices to be made. It is a minimum viable product that represents the least amount of effort to run an experiment and get feedback.[74]

Designing these prototypes in various iterations is a social, rather than a personal activity. Once the front-end analysis has been done, designing and developing a rapid prototype for an HR-centered design idea usually takes about two hours wherein a team using an established development protocol can deploy rapidly in terms of piloting and testing, and later refining the prototype.

Rapid prototyping is a design technique that can be used by global HR teams to develop innovative customer-centric services for their employees and pilot and refine them for wider deployment. It is all about being open-minded, experimenting with new solutions, and going forward with those solutions that work.

Agile management

Agile organizations developed in the 1990s in the software industry because of the need to organize IT work (especially software development) differently. Jeff Sutherland is one of its forerunners. Agile is a project management approach where detailed plans and bulky documentation makes place for flexible responses to rapidly changing circumstances and multidisciplinary teams work in short cycles to develop products and services with continuous feedback of the users.

According to McKinsey, there are five trademarks of an agile organization.[75]

- **STRATEGY**—integrated at all levels across the organization
- **STRUCTURE**—a network of empowered teams
- **PROCESS**—rapid decision making and learning cycles
- **PEOPLE**—dynamic people that ignite passion
- **TECHNOLOGY**—next-generation enabling technologies

Agile methods are being applied more and more to management in general and to HR in particular.

The four central starting points of agile working are included in the four values of the Agile Manifesto:[76]

- **INDIVIDUALS AND INTERACTIONS** over processes and tools
- **WORKING SOFTWARE** over comprehensive documentation
- **CUSTOMER COLLABORATION** over contract negotiation
- **RESPONDING TO CHANGE** over following a plan

Agile has become synonymous with flexibility to change things using self-organized teams who follow a predictable methodology while doing very little upfront planning.

Agile isn't just for tech anymore, as its methodologies are being applied to management and HR.[77] In global organizations, HR teams often work across borders to implement new initiatives whether a new benefit program or a worldwide training program. Many HR departments, especially in IT environments, are introducing "agile lite" to their own people operations. In other words, they apply the general principles of agile management without adopting all the tools and protocols from the tech world.

This approach allows them to use a simpler and faster way to respond to the needs of the users of their services. Agile project management suits small, innovative projects that are unpredictable, while traditional waterfall project management tools and techniques are better suited for those that are massive, predictable, and experience-based. Where traditional waterfall project management follows strict planning and execution, agile management is a transparent, interactive, and flexible method in which self-organized teams use very little upfront planning.[78] The main steps in "agile lite" as they can apply to HR are summarized in figure 2.

HR's traditional focus on rules-based policies and procedures and its drive for internal consistencies and equity makes adopting agile management particularly challenging for HR teams. But, in today's work environment, the focus is on innovation driven by teams. In fact, it is more important to have a good team than to hire a rock star employee. One of the conditions for individual knowledge to become a productive asset is that the individual can share that knowledge on a team in an agile way. Being able to change inside—or transform one's people management practices for the internal customer—is now a prerequisite to change the solutions outside—not falling behind with one's products and services for the external customer.

HR can use agile tools to run its own department and boost the employee experience. As Peter Cappelli and Anna Travis show in "HR goes Agile," in a *Harvard Business Review* (2018) article, many employers are already using "agile lite" methodologies in the HR realm with applications in performance appraisals, coaching, teams, compensation, recruiting, and learning and development.[79]

FIGURE 2. Description of main steps in agile project management

Main steps used in Agile by SCRUM teams	Description
Project charter	A high-level one-page narrative that includes the vision (what, how, why), the mission and the success factors.
Scrum team	Three individual team roles based on their strengths. • Scrum master—ensures the work gets done by tracking progress and removes the obstacles to optimize the team's productivity. • Product owner—empowers the connection between the team and the project's client by ensuring the deliverables meet client's expectation. • Delivery Team—delivers the product following the product owner's expectations through the completion of daily tasks.
Personas/user stories	Talk with the client (different personas or stakeholders) and understand the deliverable in a consistent format: As a <user role>, I want/need/can, etc. <goal> so that <reason>.
Product backlog	A collection of user stories that make up the wish list of the users. The list of high-level product requirements (product features and functionality) based on user stories that are implemented.
Release planning	The user stories they want to put in the release. A collection of sprints (2 to 12) broken down into manageable chunks based on the product backlog.
Sprints	A time-constrained (time-boxed) iteration milestone to build a manageable chunk of a deliverable ship-ready 100% complete product increment. Uses a three-column task board of to do, work in progress and done.
Daily scrums/ standup meetings	Daily scrums/stand-up meetings that don't exceed a time limit of 30 minutes each focused on: what did I do yesterday (what have I completed since the last meeting?); what am I doing today (what will I do before the next meeting?); and are there any obstacles in my way (what, if any, are they?).
Burndown chart	Monitors the completion of a sprint, the work that remains to be done, and the estimated completion time.
Spring retrospective	Run it by the client in regular intervals and ensure sprint reviews using tools such as starfish or race car retrospectives.

In their Dutch book, *Agile HR* (with as subtitle: the (in)dispensable role of HR in viable organizations), Willemijn Boskma, Minke Buizer, Nienke van der Hoef, Gideon Peters and Willy Zelen provide very concrete ways on how to be agile in HR. They give many insights and examples on how agile methodologies can be applied to HR.[80] This (Dutch) book is a must read to introduce agile and progressive HR practices in organizations. The authors highlight three different agile instruments (kanban, scrum, agile team portfolio management) and apply them to HR.

> **Regardless of how your HR team is organized, regardless of how large or small your organization is, you can always be agile.**

The agile tools that you choose are dependent on how far reaching you want the change to be and which approach fits your team the best.

Kanban, for example, allows you to make your regular daily task more insightful and this tool is, therefore, ideal for recruiting teams and for HR teams involved in routine process work with many operational tasks. *Kanban* is the Japanese word for visual board. Such a board, usually with four columns—to do, busy, done, waiting— is placed centrally in the workspace and gives each team member an ongoing up-to-date overview of where things stand.

Scrum, another agile tool, is ideal for change management teams working on a specific improvement project with concrete objectives, budget, and deadlines. Scrum teams always are multi-disciplinary and work in close consultation with the client. They add value because of the quick feedback and ability to be agile. In scrum, there are three roles:

- **SCRUM TEAM**: A multidisciplinary team made up of 6 to 7 team members who work in a self-organized manner. They deliver the product through the completion of daily tasks.
- **PRODUCT OWNER**: Empowers the connection between the team and the project's client by ensuring the deliverables meet the client's expectations. The product owner guards the client order, determines priorities, and makes decisions.
- **SCRUM MASTER**: Facilitates the scrum team and is responsible for the quality of the process. The scrum master ensures the work gets done by tracking progress and removes the obstacles to optimize the team's productivity.

And, there are four specific ceremonies in agile (sprint planning, stand-up meeting, review, and retrospective) that divide the lead time in shorter time periods, also called sprints. This allows for very quick, deliverable products and these intermediate deliverables are very tangible. Every sprint starts with sprint planning where the scrum team determines what the goal is, which results need to be attained, and how they will be attained. During the sprint period there are daily stand-up meetings lasting no more than 15 minutes where team members brief each other on the work in progress. There is a short client review where colleagues are invited. Lastly, the last ceremony is the retrospective where the team reflects on the whole process. Scrum can, for example, be applied in HR to a new recruiting technique or the development and testing of a new onboarding program.

Agile team portfolio management (also called Agile TPM) is a third agile management tool that is ideal to engage teams who work on different projects simultaneously. For example, a complex change management initiative or talent development program that demands more preparatory work to implement, Agile TPM allows the entire project team (or multiple agile teams) to stay current on the status of each other's work, make quick decisions, as well as timely adaptations and changes.

One of the biggest challenges implementing agile is the reward system. For example, individual salary scales and rewards can be decoupled from the function and substituted by group valuation rewards linked to the capacity of both the employee and/or the team. Or, it is possible to make a distinction between the fixed salary and flexible performance bonus, detached from the annual budget and not considered a personnel expense. The reward system is always the last to change, but it is crucial to include this subject in the initial conversations with the different stakeholders around agile projects.

Managers will likely not disappear with the increasing use of agile and self-managed teams. However, managers will have a different role and become more of a team coach. HR will need to make sure these managers know how to work in agile teams and develop the right leadership skills.

Supplementing the *Agile Manifesto*, there is also an *Agile HR Manifesto* with values to guide the use of agile HR in organizations.[81]

- **COLLABORATIVE NETWORKS** over hierarchical structures
- **TRANSPARENCY** over secrecy
- **ADAPTABILITY** over prescriptiveness
- **INSPIRATION AND ENGAGEMENT** over management and retention
- **INTRINSIC MOTIVATION** over extrinsic rewards
- **AMBITION** over obligation

How do we get to work concretely with agile lite in HR?

HR can augment its long-term strategic workforce planning with more frequent operational planning meetings using shorter cycles—twice a year, or each quarter, rather than annually. Today, it is impossible to accurately predict how many workers an employer will need five years from now and which roles workers will assume.

Another application of an agile approach in recruiting is to emphasize who the applicant is and where the candidate wants to go, rather than look at what the person did in the past. Agile organizations prefer to search for T-shaped candidate profiles, whose added value for the organization lies beyond their current expertise (we discuss this in chapter 5), and learnatics (who we described in chapter 3). In agile recruiting, learning agility is often of greater worth than a formal degree or years of experience. Your employer brand can also benefit when interactions with (potential) employees are faster and your brand can be adjusted quicker.

In learning and development, it behooves HR—if they want to work in agile—to do away with Personal Improvement Plans (PIPs) and substitute them with regular real-time feedback and coaching conversations with employees using a limited number of questions. The employee must reflect on their own work asking: Am I doing things right? Am I doing the right things? What are my strengths? Am I in the right place? What will I do to further develop myself. You can even install an ambition board where employees share their ambitions or install a wall of failure, where mistakes made are shared with the intention of learning from each other.

While agile is all about the use of scrum teams, sprint, *kanban* and other tools, it is also a combination of a way of thinking and doing and to address projects in a flexible manner, leading to an agile and customer-oriented organization.

Behavioral economics

Neoclassic economic theories are being supplanted by behavioral economics (the combination of psychology and economics), an off-shoot of heterodox economics.[82] Whereas the conventional economic model posits that people act as rational, self-interested agents concerned with maximizing utility, behavioral economics challenges this economic rationality with the idea that people act as humans (thinking automatically) rather than economic actors (thinking reflectively).[83]

HR can find many insights in the life-long work of Daniel Kahneman and Amos Tzervsky on decision making.[84] System I and System II thinking refer to two cognitive systems or modes of thinking. System II thinking is aligned with conventional economic models in which decision making is rule-bound, rational, deliberate, and self-aware.

It is the controlled way of thinking best summarized by the words slow and deliberate. System I thinking is aligned with the behavioral economic model in which decision making is intuitive, instinctive, and uncontrolled. In contrast to the reflective and conscious mode of System II thinking, System I thinking is rapid and automatic.

In a nutshell, System I thinking is automatic, fast, intuitive, instinctive, effortless, based on gut reaction, uncontrolled, unconscious skilled, and uses associative thinking while System II thinking is reflective, slow, rational, self-conscious, an effortful mental activity, using conscious thought, controlled, self-aware, rule following, and a combination of deductive/inductive thinking.

Although most people toggle back and forth between System I and System II thinking depending on circumstances, human nature is not purely rational. It is bound by three distinct traits:

- **BOUNDED RATIONALITY** (constraints in our available information, time, and capacity to think leading to the adoption of heuristics/rules of thumb).
- **BOUNDED WILLPOWER** (people will take actions despite conflicts with their long-term goals and interests).
- **BOUNDED SELF-INTEREST** (people are affected by factors beyond their economic self-interest and are often willing to sacrifice their own self-interest to help others).[85]

These psychological traits at the roots of our judgments should inform HR practices, policies, and programs. In recognizing our bounded rationality, willpower, and self-interest, behavioral economics can inform HR practices to reduce the unconscious bias in decision-making.

> **By being aware of common heuristics and biases, we can develop an architecture and use behavioral nudging—a small push in the right direction—to allow people to make desired decisions that are better, healthier, and safer.[86]**

In other words, the way HR present choices to its employees has an enormous impact on the decisions they will make. In the public government sector, marketing and creative professionals have used such choice architecture to guide consumers in their choices.

HEURISTICS AND BIASES

We are all very, very busy. We simply do not have the time to think everything through and analyze each decision in depth. Instead, we rely on rules of thumb or heuristics. In other words, people do not make decisions based on complete and reliable information. Instead of attempting the impossible—deliberately analyzing and thinking of everything (using reflective System II thinking), we use simple rules of thumb or heuristics to make quick decisions (using automatic System I thinking).

Below is a short description of a few heuristics that have been identified:[87]

- **ANCHORING**—people tend to "anchor" the value of something based on their first exposure to a number, starting with some known number and adjusting in the direction they think is appropriate. For example, the number of hours it usually takes to complete a task for a particular project that is acceptable (and feasible), gives employees an anchor for orientation. People can be influenced in a subtle way by giving them an starting point (or anchor) for their thought process.
- **AVAILABILITY**—people assess the likelihood of risk by how readily examples come to mind. If they can easily think of relevant examples, they are far more likely to be frightened and concerned than if they cannot. For example, if someone who has experienced a layoff in the past, they will perceive their chances of being laid off again much higher than someone who has never been fired. People tend to judge risk higher than the actual occurrence of events if they recall such an event, but the probability of risk is distorted for those who can't recall such a concrete event.
- **REPRESENTATIVENESS**—the likelihood that A belongs to B is judged by how similar A is to their image or stereotype of B (misperception of randomness). While stereotypes often have a kernel of truth, prejudices can creep in when comparability and frequency deviate. This often happens when certain characteristics of diverse co-workers are judged in a stereotypical manner.
- **FRAMING**—the way things are framed leads people to different conclusions. Framing works because people tend to be lazy and passive decision makers. This means that management can be a powerful push in the right direction. Yet, sometimes they fool employees by presenting their company's information through inappropriate framing.
- **LOSS AVERSION**—people avoid decisions that will lead to loss. People hate losing and our automatic system can react very emotionally to losses. We feel miserable when we lose and happy when we win. As a result, people will tend to make decisions that avoid losses. Loss aversion can also be a nudge that pushes us to resist change, even if the change is in our benefit.

The fact that people make decisions in the ways described above has consequences for the behavior of employees. However, HR also uses these heuristics in recruitment, selection, performance management, benefits, and other practices. HR must become aware that they— just like anyone else—are subject to their own unconscious biases.

There are many HR examples where (un)conscious biases can creep in. For example, HR can reduce the selection bias by eliminating the applicant's name (and other personal information) on CVs and application forms when they present the candidates to managers or can opt for replacing the human selection process with artificial intelligence (representativeness). HR also should avoid providing benefits that may be too generous that need to be rescinded (loss aversion). It is better to let employees choose from a series of fixed benefits that are sustainable. HR can also frame information by presenting it in a more positive manner where the focus lies on the opportunity (framing). Regarding performance management, HR can anchor a performance goals by setting it high yet realistic and attainable. The same can be applied to salary negotiations in recruiting or response options in a employee survey (anchoring).

CHOICE ARCHITECTURE

As mentioned before, people make countless choices every day. If we had think consciously about all these choices, we would barely get things done. Most choices we make are automatic, intuitive, and impulsive. Nudging takes advantage of this through a choice architecture.

A choice architecture manipulates the way people make decisions by organizing the context in which they do so. While keeping the freedom of choice, people are nudged towards the desired choice. Usually only a limited set of choices is created allowing for better decision making.[88]

Much like the parent who offers a child several choices in snacks, all of them healthy, a choice architect utilizes a form of libertarian paternalism that allows for freedom of choice in a paternalistic way that better assures good behavioral decisions. In progressive companies, HR focuses on developing choice architecture that aligns with their organizational culture to influence employees to live longer, healthier, and better lives. For example, in the cafeteria of your workplace, healthy snacks can placed at eye level and less healthy candy at the bottom or at the top so they are less obvious. You still give people a choice, but you make less easy for them to make the designated choice rather than the desired choice. Of course, one could remove unhealthy snacks in the workplace all together!

The role HR plays in designing the context of employee decision making in progressive companies is captured by Thaler and Sunstein: "Choice architects can make major improvements to the lives of others by designing user-friendly environments."[89]

NUDGING

One aspect of choice architecture is nudging. In the English language a nudge is a gentle push in order to draw someone's attention. Nudging utilizes cheap and easy interventions to change behavior in predictable ways without forbidding any options, and without changing economic incentives significantly.[90]

Typically, people's behavior is regulated through laws, regulations, policies, information, and even financial incentives. However, these methods are not always successful and can be rather expensive. People do not always make rational choices to follow the rules or act in their best interest.

Thaler and Sunstein, the authors of *Behavioral Nudging* propose that by appropriately implementing incentives and nudges, we may be able to enhance people's lives and solve some of society's major problems.[91]

Many biases in decision making present opportunities for HR to nudge themselves, co-workers, and employees towards making more appropriate decisions for themselves and the organization. Nudging can also be used in large HR transformation and change management projects. Imagine that your organization wants to introduce a new way to cooperate between the silos, share knowledge, or stimulate people from different departments to better support each other. The physical environment is open, transparent with different types of workspaces and opportunities for informal consultation. Your employees find this new office layout nice but have problems working in this new environment. They prefer to work as they have always done. This is not necessarily because they don't want to but their decisions and behavior have become automated. We are creatures of habit and have difficulties changing our behavior. It requires time and intensive support. Appealing to common sense and reason may be insufficient. To really change, people may need to be nudged a bit. When changing processes, it is possible to seduce employees to work in a different way by concrete interventions in the workplace and finding an appropriate nudge. HR can nudge employees to take the stairs rather than the elevator by simply placing strips on the ground. It is amazing how small changes in the physical environment can lead to behavioral change.

HR analytics

HR analytics refers to the utilization of organizational data, external data, and HR data to meet employee needs (or soft HRM) as well as hard HRM needs such as strategic decision making. There are many technical terms involved, such as data warehousing (smart saving of available data) and business intelligence (making company and other data actionable). Data used in hard HRM is organized, analyzed, and presented in a meaningful way through statistical techniques that allow for prediction.[92] In order to be effectively implemented, HR analytics requires organizations to support their talent management decisions with data and then measure the effectiveness, efficiency, and impact of those decisions.[93]

In deploying HR analytics, HR must first formulate a relevant research question. Then, it goes through four distinct phases:

- **SCOPE THE PROJECT**—identify a feasible project and understand the capabilities and limitations of the organizational data, link it to organizational objectives, identify the research question and design, and then identify the type and source of data required.
- **ASSEMBLE THE TEAM**—identify members of the core team who have analytical interests and capabilities, identify the stakeholders and decision-makers, then galvanize them with the knowledge of the importance and limitations of the data.
- **MANAGE THE DATA**—acquire, protect, analyze, interpret, and present the results of the data visually.
- **TAKE STRATEGIC ACTION**—present and discuss the evidence-based results to stakeholders, suggest managerial action, and participate in evidence-based decision-making based on results.

Finally, evaluate the impact of these decisions on both the organization and HR itself. The value of HR analytics to talent management practices throughout the HR life cycle has been well documented.

> **Tracking things enables one to find patterns and themes in the data and identify hotspots that require action.**

Measuring and tracking human behavior requires the use of qualitative as well as quantitative tools. A number of analytical techniques such as data mining, sentiment analysis and A/B testing are being increasingly applied to HR to guide talent management decisions.

DATA MINING

Datamining extracts and examines data from a large database. For example, HR can examining patterns in the data of its HRIS as it applies to various HR functions over the life cycle of an employee, or mining of a vendor they use (such as benefits, expense report management, travel data, etc.) to identify specific trends and utilization patterns. Using large quantities of past enterprise data allows HR to make not only better data-driven decisions, but also build more predictable models.

In *Better People Analytics* (*Harvard Business Review*, November-December 2018) Paul Leonardi and Noshir Contractor argue for better people analytics. They propose that rather than simply mining the attributes of employees, the people's interactions are equally if not more important. They argue for the use of relational analytics to examine—what they call the digital exhaust of a company—and find structural signatures in social networks (as mined in e-mail exchanges, chats, file transfers, etc.).[94]

SENTIMENT ANALYSIS

Sentiment analysis consists of using either pulse surveys or text analytics to mine various sources of data for employee opinions or sentiment. The data is usually collected from emails, various social media platforms and the Internet in an ambient way or by asking a sentiment question on a sample of the workforce on a regular basis.

This method is not new and has been in use in marketing (customer sentiment) and academic circles to predict trends and election results.

Sentiment analysis allows HR to use social networks across the company, identify and measure employee emotions, motivations, and engagement and better understand work-related attitudinal and behavioral aspects of the employees. It helps measure cultural change and gather data if what your organization is doing works for different employee groups.

The use of sentiment data provided by employees—whether in an ambient or self-reported manner—carries with it many issues when it comes to the privacy of employee data even if the data is company owned.

A/B TESTING

A/B testing compares two variants (A and B) of a modality to see which one performs better. Such testing is commonly used in market research where potential customers are divided in two groups and each group is presented with a different option to see which one is more attractive. HR can also test the attractiveness of different modalities of various rewards or compare employee satisfaction with various HR touchpoints.

In A/B testing two different modalities are compared. A is the "control," usually the current system that is considered the champion. B is the treatment or challenger—a modification of something we are trying to test or improve. In a small-scale experiment, users are randomly assigned to either group A or B. Metrics that determine the success of the intervention are calculated and compared until sufficient (statistically significant) evidence is gathered to determine whether the decision to introduce a new modality is a good or bad decision. With this kind of experiment, HR can come to a conclusion in a more sustainable and evidence-based way to implement a change inititative.[95]

By using data, HR can, for example, determine the employee experience of certain subgroups of employees—based on their demographics—is dependent on certain secondary working conditions and intervene. While the topic of HR analytics has gained in popularity in the academic and professional HR literature, many companies are not utilizing its potential. This is unfortunate because when data experts from outside of HR are invited to join the team, they bring a new perspective on the data and their analysis and insights allows HR to make more evidence-based decisions. HR analytics can add value and be an effective alternative to existing HR reports and metrics.

Global standardization and local responsiveness

A key part of HR's role as architect in designing employee experiences is ensuring that its practices align with the culture of its geographic workplace and workforce. While every company must ensure some level of standardization in HR processes and procedures that apply to all employees, legal compliance and standardization must be balanced with sensitivity to the local cultural norms and account for the diversity of the employees. The global (standardization) and local (responsiveness) discussion is embedded in duality theory where global organizations are compelled to standardize to take advantage of the economies of scale, yet must localize to comply with local laws and meet local cultural acceptability requirements.[96]

Additional heuristics are often used as well when deciding whether to design global (standardized) or local (localized) HR processes. One may standardize the HR principle but localize the implementation of the practice; standardize the upstream process, but localize the downstream HR process flowing to the employee.

There are many examples of the localization of HR practices—which becomes a must because of the culture, structure, and legal systems in the different countries where a company operates: what does the concept of many HR practices—such as of diversity, rewards, engagement, teamwork, and other management practices—mean in different cultures and how do we operationalize (or measure) these practices in the local context?

The automation of many transactional HR activities (with little added value) creates an opportunity to be involved in more strategic HR work. This requires a new set of competencies and skills that supplement and/or complement the existing HR skill set.

> **Armed with a new *#ZigZagHR*-Stack, HR practitioners can move up to a position where they are more than just HR experts.**

This has allowed non-HR leaders to learn about HR concepts and philosophies and enter into a partnership with stakeholders (senior management, line management and employees) about the true culture of their organization.

Progressive organizations are evolving towards a new context where all managers have a common strategic HR vision with regard to teamwork, development, engagement, rewards, and other people-based matters within their own function. Publications and blogs frequently read by business leaders, like the *Wall Street Journal*, the *Financial Times*, and the *Harvard Business Review*, feature many more HR-related articles when comparing today to a decade ago and the topics covered are often becoming water-cooler conversation. Various HR networks on LinkedIn—whether personal or vendor-related—have also broadened the discussion on HR trends and innovative practices.

HR must understand and leverage the *#ZigZagHR*-Stack and develop innovative practices that are aligned with the new world of work and the worker and operate in a sweet spot where what's good for the workforce is also good for the employee.

IN SUMMARY

Demographics, technology and globalization have created disruption with tremendous implications for how we work, the kind of work we do, and who our coworkers in the organization are. This presents a unique set of opportunities and challenges for HR in terms of reinventing and reengineering their role and where they add value. In spite of the HR disruption, the automation of some of the HR transactional functions (low value-added activities) will force HR to become more strategic and become aligned with the business. This is a new skill set for HR. The core question now becomes: where can HR (not) add (more) value in this new constellation? HR professionals must complement their base HR competencies with skills and tools from other management disciplines and adopt an augmented #ZigZagHR-Stack that includes design thinking (strategy), behavioral economics (where psychology and economics meet), agile management (flexible project management), and analytics (data analysis and management science).

5

#ZigZagHR
Careers

HR MUST CHANGE INSIDE TO
RESPOND TO DEMANDS FOR
SOLUTIONS OUTIDE

5

If HR wants to play a proactive role, it will have to fundamentally reinvent itself. This requires an arsenal of new competencies (*#ZigZagHR*-Stack), but also an innovative and mindset (*#ZigZagHR*-Ecosystem). In this chapter *#ZigZagHR*-Careers, we first zoom in on HR as a management discipline, its evolution, and the many challenges it faces today.

We must reinvent HR

Some progressive companies have taken the lead and already disrupted their dominant HR thinking, policies, and practices as a result of the demands of the outside world and have come up with new people management solutions inside their organizations. It is clear that HR must change inside to respond to demands for solutions outside. Demanding that we partially obliterate ourselves before we are being left behind is a tall order! But reinvention of HR must come from within—even if the solutions we must adopt may be difficult. A shift in HR approach is existential for HR survival and required for organizational success. Progressive HR practices should not just be equated with start-up companies who do not have the burden of legacy HR systems. HR practitioners must ask the hard questions, be forward thinking and innovate—in other words lead the change in an agile manner.

We are not simply thinking about band-aid solutions or incremental changes to HR as this would have the same effect of rearranging the chairs on the deck of the sinking Titanic! HR practitioners must practice the three-box approach proposed by Vijay Govindarajan and Chris Trimble (*Harvard Business Review*, 2011) on itself. It must decide what to continue because it currently adds value and improves the performance of the business (box 1). It must overcome its own dominant logic of how it does things today and identify what to destroy because it is no longer relevant (box 2). Finally, it must create new and truly innovative processes that fundamentally change the people business and add value to both the workforce and the organization (box 3).[97]

As we have argued, existing competencies and practices must be supplemented with management knowledge, tools, and technologies from other disciplines as we described in chapter 4 as the #ZigZagHR-Stack. There is an urgent need for cross-fertilization and to break down the many silos in our organizations. This makes practicing #ZigZagHR even more relevant.

HR: Sub-silo in a silo

HR as a management discipline has evolved over the past decades. It is stratified into broad categories such as hard and soft HR, transactional and strategic HR, and further siloed into various subdisciplines (strategic HR, workforce planning, recruitment and selection, compensation and benefits, performance management, learning and development, industrial relations, etc.) each with a core HR body of knowledge (HR BoK).

One of the basic principles of this HR reinvention lies within the mindset of HR practitioners and their willingness to continuously develop themselves.

We must realize that what once was considered the HR domain no longer is sufficient to add value to our organizations and their stakeholders.

Over the past decade, through the strategic work of Dave Ulrich and Wayne Brockbank, who developed the leading competency models for those working in HR, an HR BoK has developed as an academic subject matter as well as a set of applied practitioner-oriented policies and practices.[98]

In the US, Canada, and the United Kingdom, HR professional societies have further codified these competencies and developed certification programs to benchmark that practitioners had baseline practice ability.

It is fair to say that, compared to other professions, HR has a very low professionalization profile because of its T-shaped knowledge base. There lies the fact there are no barriers to entry into the HR role and it is no longer clearcut who the HR customer really is.

Specialist, generalist, or stuck in the middle?

The HR Bok is derived from disciplines (such as psychology, sociology and law) and requires incumbents to have baseline knowledge of a number of business disciplines (accounting, finance, marketing, operations, management, data analysis, and strategy) to become a legitimate business partner.

The first reason why HR has such a low professionalization profile has to do with the fact that HR is either too narrow in scope or has siloed knowledge. HR practitioners tend to either be generalists (have breadth but no depth; jack of all trades but master of none, or dash-shaped) or specialist (have depth but no breadth, or I-shaped). This keeps them doing mainly transactional activities—that are stifling, control-oriented, and add limited value to the organization—or specialized HR activities such as benefits administration, payroll, labor relations, and employment law that tend to be administrative and compliance-oriented.

They are what Herzberg labels "hygiene factors" in his motivation theory[99]—they must be done at a certain level of excellence, but they do not really add value. It is these HR activities that are likely to be taken over by artificial intelligence and algorithms. There is already plenty of evidence in progressive HR companies today how these HR transactional activities are done via shared service centers (with mixed results), chatbots, the use of other non-human Information Communication Technology (ICT) tools, and self-managed by the worker through IT systems and apps.

The competencies of a CHRO role (Chief Human Resource Officer) or HR director are both T-shaped—specialist but also generalist in other areas of expertise—and M-shaped[100]—understanding the depth of multiple pillars that contribute to HR effectiveness and being able to manage and integrate them so they can be used to align the workforce in support of the strategic objectives of the organization. Surprisingly, many successful CHROs are recruited from outside of the HR domain and have brought their enterprise and global experience from other disciplines with them. It is also striking that many of the "new" HR innovations and strategic initiatives are being propagated by HR consultants who have no HR domain experience—whether it relates to analytics, IT and software applications, employee experience, letting go of organizational control, and others.

Stuck in the middle, HR practitioners in the trenches often feel overburdened by the successive new idea *du jour* they are bombarded with at HR conferences, blogs and publications. They are expected to apply these attractive and often lofty propositions and new requirements in the specific context of their workplace. There, they are likely to encounter a confronting reality, without specific training, buy-in from others, or resources. In the mean time, they must continue to assume their transactional and compliance-focused HR activities at high levels of excellence all the while being seduced by trendy new apps, new theories, models, and tools that are cheered upon and now expected in their work environment.

To be fair, when HR bashing is done, it is usually directed at the limited views of HR generalists and specialists who add perhaps little value to their stakeholders rather than the integrated HR practices that progressive companies have developed. It behooves all HR practitioners to acquire new competencies and reinvent their role. That's what we advocated in the *#ZigZagHR*-Stack chapter.

Anyone can do HR, right?

The hallmark of a "true" profession is that incumbents not only have a great deal of discretionary autonomy—based on a specialized body of knowledge acquired through higher education, an ethical code of conduct, and a license to practice regulated by a professional organization—but they can exclude members who do not have the above credentials from practicing. Only a few countries in the world have recognized HR certification credentials (UK, Canada, US). Although they are aiming for a worldwide reach, certification remains, so far, mainly an Anglo-Saxon matter. But the fact there are virtually no thresholds to enter HR, anyone can easily enter the field and/or influence who takes on these managerial HR roles in companies. Especially at the senior HR level, we often see talented people from outside the HR domain taken over as CHROs. That is the second reason why HR has a low professionalization profile.

We often hear "everybody is in HR." Actually, everybody independent of one's role is co-responsible for people management. Instead of saying, "everybody is in HR," perhaps we should argue that "everybody should do HR."

Help! Who is really the customer?

A third reason for the low professionalization profile of HR has to do with the fact that it is no longer clear who HR's primary customer is. In the same way that it is important for an organization to know who their external customers are, it is important for HR to ask itself that same question. Knowledge of the customer is a requirement to get focus on one's purpose. As HR evolved to respond simultaneously to external changes and meet internal demands, identification of who the primary HR customer is got lost.

HR has multiple stakeholders with the primary ones being the employee, the managers, and the company. But, it also works with many other stakeholders such as the unions, regulatory agencies, and educational institutions. These stakeholders not only have different requirements but may also have different within-group interests. It is HR's role to balance these different requirements within the organization and find a sustainability sweet spot—namely what is good for one stakeholder (e.g., the employee or union) is also good for the others (e.g., the interests of the organization and legal compliance). Many HR practices (including downsizing, offshoring, outsourcing, executive compensation, sexual harassment, discrimination, investigations, etc.) have given the worker the perception that perhaps HR has lost the "H" in HR.[101] Instead, it has become the protector of the status of the organization rather than meeting the needs of employees.

In addition, many employers work with workers who have very diverse employment statuses (think freelancers, subcontractors, and other flexible workers), which raises questions regarding which role HR can and must play for the people who are non-employees.

The new HR challenges

Important scientific discoveries usually emerge from scientist, who deviate from calibrated paths. They get new insights because they look at a situation from another point of view. Hence, they make connections that produce far-reaching changes in their patterns of thinking. Thomas Kühn in his 1962 book, *The Structure of Scientific*

Revolutions, called this a paradigm shift. A change of paradigm or paradigm shift occurs when people reject an existing paradigm (commonly accepted way of thinking) and embrace a different one, resulting in a totally different approach and the formulation of new questions.[102]

#In developing the next HR paradigm, we look at the challenges brought about by a rapidly growing, non-traditional workforce employment model; the impact of artificial intelligence and machine learning on HR practice; the need to acquire a growth mindset; and the needed pendulum swing in HR from control to trust.

The new employment model

In the traditional employment model, organizations hire their talent as employees or outsource an entire business process to a contractor. In this "make vs. buy" model, HR manages the various stages of the employee life cycle under the broader umbrella of a legal framework, cultural practices, and an implied social contract between the employer and the employee. As discussed in *#ZigZag*-Workforce, a non-traditional employment model is emerging today—side-by-side with the traditional model—and rapidly expects to become the dominant model in the future. The non-traditional employment model juxtaposes "employees" to "non-employees." Non-employees fall under a variety of workforce modalities and a wide spectrum of work arrangements such as on-demand workers, contingent workers, independent contractors, project-based workers, freelance workers, gig economy workers, and temporary workers.

> The growth of the non-traditional workforce sector—soon to be the mainstream modality of work—is driven by both personal and organizational needs.

A segment of the workforce is looking for greater flexibility and control over when, where, and how to work and their life in general. Employers are looking at more agile ways to use talent and reduce overall employment costs. As we discussed already in chapter 3, the new employment classification of workers (employee versus non-employee; traditional versus non-traditional workforce) has a number of interrelated challenges for HR. What is the correct employment status? How do we manage a blended workforce? What are adequate compensation and benefits?

Important discoveries often happen in science when researchers deviate from calibrated paths.

Customized work relations

The employee and worker experience with an organization, as Jacob Morgan states, is mainly influenced by the physical environment, the organizational culture, and the technological tools.[103] It is also mediated by the diverse personas of individual workers. Hence, HR must aim to customize the worker experiences according to the needs of the incumbents based on their stage in life, preferences, personalities, workstyles and their diverse ascribed and achieved characteristics. This is a tall order for HR whose work has been driven and focused on standardized, one-size-fits-all HR policies and practices that by being equal are thought to be equitable and fair. In addition, the one-size-fits-all working relationship–where everyone is an employee and co-located in the employer's workspace—does not necessarily apply when workers (whether employees or freelancers) are no longer physically working side-by-side but perform remote work. How does HR manage work relations when one works at home, the other in a satellite office or workspace, or in another country or even continent?

HR is truly becoming both the architect of the culture and its talent. These new employment opportunities impact HR and we must look for new angles and approaches regarding the culture and structure of the organization, including the HR organization itself. HR will, on one hand, have less employees on the payroll and, on the other hand, have new challenges in serving a workforce that is no longer made up of employees and both, employees and contract workers, will increasingly work remotely.

Artificial intelligence, machine learning, and HR

There is a great deal of fear and anxiety around artificial intelligence and machine learning and its impact on work. HR work is not immune to this. With artificial intelligence developing algorithms that allow employees to use an HR self-service model, HR can then use its capabilities elsewhere and relegate the burdensome, transactional activities to machines.

HR work without human intervention? In theory, this is already possible. Many such HR without human intervention activities are already being used to recruit people: using a chatbox for answers to HR questions; listening systems and sentiment analysis to keep the pulse on worker engagement; tracking and measuring human behavior quantitatively and qualitatively to discover patterns and themes that can be acted upon.

Artificial intelligence is not a faraway utopia or (no longer) dystopic science fiction, although, we must admit the HR self-service model transformation is in many ways still in its infancy. This does not take away from the fact that progressive companies using these tools in HR are looking for ways to scale up these systems without losing human interaction as the critical mass of leaders, managers, and workers must still feel like they have an HR person to turn to.

In the meantime, the employee pool is shrinking relative to gig economy/freelance workers. Will this result in HR shrinking as well if they focus on employees only? Also, think about the many HR transactional tasks that are (and will be) taken over by artificial intelligence and machine learning. Organizations should rethink the HR-to-staff ratio rule of thumb of 1:100 (1 FTE human resource for every 100 employees). In the past, a common benchmark for HR staffing has usually been the HR-to-employee-ratio or the number of HR full-time equivalent positions (working in HR generalist and specialist roles—excluding payroll and learning & development) divided by the total number of full-time equivalent employees (x 100). Average HR-to-employee ratios usually decline when the size of the employer increases. It is not difficult to see that this formula becomes problematic when an employer uses a blended workforce and non-traditional workers working side-by-side with employees. With fewer employees and more automated HR services, the resulting HR-to-employee ratio is likely to dramatically cut the staffing of HR departments.

What does #ZigZagHR mean for HR careers?

The good news is that HR is no longer the side show, it is now the show! Finding and attracting the right talent is what preoccupies any organization today since one of greatest enterprise people risks of organizations today is not having the talent needed to grow one's company and/or staying at the edge of innovation due to lack of people imagination. HR must mine for talent, internally and externally, and piece together a structure and culture where people thrive. Once on board, HR must create an environment and culture where collaboration and connectedness—the new expectations of the workplace—are embedded in its organizational DNA and reflected in the day-to-day activities of the workforce. But foremost, HR must work on staying relevant.

Internal pressures from employees is forcing companies—large and small—to quickly address workplace problems as employees are increasingly sharing their discontent around experiences on social media and other sites, which has an impact on the employer brand and employer value proposition.

> For HR to stay relevant; it requires a growth mindset rather than being stuck on a fixed mindset; letting go of control by fostering trust; breaking down the silos within HR and between other management disciplines; and adding value to the business. HR must demolish the silos within HR and the walls with other management departments.

The good news is that HR is no longer the side show! Finding, attracting, and retaining the right talent is the primary preoccupation of any organization.

From a fixed HR-mindset to a growth HR mindset

In her book, *Mindset: The Psychology of Success*, Carol Dweck distinguishes between a fixed mindset (intelligence is static—a more deterministic view of the world) and a growth mindset (intelligence can be developed—a greater sense of free will). A fixed mindset leads to a desire to look smart and therefore a tendency to avoid challenges, to give up easily when obstacles are encountered; to see effort as fruitless; to ignore useful negative feedback; and to feel threatened by the success of others. As a result, people with a fixed mindset may plateau early and achieve less than their full potential. A growth mindset leads to a desire to learn, and therefore a tendency to embrace challenge; to persist in the face of setbacks and obstacles; to see effort as the path to mastery; to learn from criticism; and to find lessons and inspiration in the success of others. As a result, they achieve ever higher levels of achievement.[104]

To be successful at *#ZigZagHR*, a practitioner must ask: what is the extent of my fixed mindset in my current HR work? What am I stuck on in HR that stands in the way of the full potential of people?

#ZigZagHR is not a zero-sum game

Fueled by a growing millennial generation in the workforce that values teamwork, transparency and flexibility, some progressive companies have transformed their HR practices (such as annual performance appraisals, rigid work rules, expense reimbursements, management approvals, etc.) by creating a culture of trust and collaboration instead of controlling for the occasional "bad apple." This is a major shift for HR to let go of control (the ultimate compliance tool) and create a more supportive environment.

In a 2018 *Harvard Business Review* article entitled "Structure That's not Stifling," Ranjay Gulati argues that employee freedom and operational control are not a zero-sum and should not be viewed as two extremes.[105] With a zero-sum or fixed sum game the interests of both parties are opposite of each other and the gain of one is the loss of the other. According to Gulati, that should not be the case. Instead, employee freedom and empowerment must be embedded in an organizational framework of purpose, priority and principles that provide employees with a living set of guidelines. Purpose is a single shared goal that sums up the "why" of the organization. Priorities are the behavioral rules that reflect these organizational goals. Principles are the practical, reasonable options in day-to-day work.

Rather than attempting to control and regulate behaviors, employees should have "freedom within a framework." This framework must be supported with substantive resources (including onboarding, training, development, managerial support, etc.) so that employees can understand the limits of their freedom and exercise freedom with responsibilities. This allows for a hands-off approach where employees are trusted rather than controlled and can do their best work.

Break the HR and management disciplinary silos

In progressive organizations, HR is the architecture of talent and organizational culture. It builds a people management team that can integrate knowledge outside of the HR domain into the people practices. The role, composition, and competencies of the integrated people management teams in successful organizations is now often composed of at least four different players that contribute to make new people management stick, and only one of them is someone from the HR domain. For example, the organization of People Operations at Google seems to innovate as much on people issues as they do on technology. To manage its continued expansion and growth while maintaining its people principles, Google designed a three-tiered talent model for People Operations. One-third is comprised of people with an HR background and HR skill set. One-third comes from boutique and large management consulting companies who have an aptitude for team and management problem solving. One-third shares an analytical background as statisticians or organizational psychologists, focusing on patterns, data analysis, and other analytics to improve practices for higher ROI.[106]

The new composition of the people management team has engendered a new slew of "people management" (read HR) job titles. These new job titles already reflect the evolution of HR while older, more familiar titles are used less and less. New titles that have emerged are: vice president or director of people (or people operations), DIBs, people analytics, chief happiness officer, vibe manager, field HR manager, team success, employee engagement, and coach. These titles show the far-reaching change in the role and contribution of HR.[107]

In progressive organizations, HR is the architect of talent and organizational culture— they build HR teams who can integrate outside knowledge in their own operations.

Add value to the business

Progressive HR practices are agile, transparent, data driven and subject to experimentation and testing to show they really work or achieve the intended goals. These practices are continuously improved to meet the needs of all the stakeholders.

Progressive *#ZigZagHR* practices that add value to the business are based on a three-legged stool where successful people practices require adequate conceptualization, operationalization, and implementation. Every HR decision must be supported by critical thinking, analysis, and execution. Let's illustrate this with the practice of diversity, which is now an existential requirement for organizational innovation. First, there must be a solid exploration of what diversity, inclusion, and belonging—or DIBs—mean for a particular organization. Second, the concepts must be operationalized. Namely how do I measure the success or failure—efficiency, effectiveness, and impact—of the people initiative around this? Finally, how do I implement these DIBs initiatives as a global-local standard in my company and make it stick? Progressive HR practices are agile and data-driven, subject to experimentation and testing to see whether they work, meet intended objectives, and can be improved to meet stakeholder needs.

#ZigZagHR-Careers are taking on different shapes whether in career tracks, employment status, HR titles and competencies to operate in an agile way. A global ecosystem of progressive HR practices and practitioners is growing outside of the normal professional channels. Whether we call it HR or by any other name, progressive *#ZigZagHR* careers are breaking down the traditional route into making the talent work for all involved.

To use a famous line of inquiry for managerial decisions used at Amazon and popularized by its CEO, Jeff Bezos, HR must focus on exploring the "dogs not barking" rather than continue business as usual. A dog not barking is not a problem today (whether real or perceived), but will be a big problem tomorrow if nothing is done. A *#ZigZag* shift in HR's approach is essential for its survival and required for organizational success.

Progressive *#ZigZagHR* practices that add value to the business are based on the three-legged stool where successful people practices require adequate conceptualization, operationalization, and implementation.

IN SUMMARY

Just like any other type of professional work, HR is not immune to disruption. Lessons learned from the turmoil of reengineering in the 1990s—where many HR people laid off waves of employees to ultimately be laid off themselves—suggest that HR can take a proactive leadership role by disrupting its own paradigm. This requires not only a new way of thinking about enterprise people risk and worker value, but also putting an expanded set of competencies to use in an integrative and collaborative manner.

6

#ZigZagHR-
Activities

HOW HR *ZIGZAGS* BETWEEN TRADITIONAL AND PROGRESSIVE HR PRACTICES

6

In the new context of work and the worker, HR must make a number of operational decisions to add sustained value to the people management function for employers and the workforce alike. In doing so, HR must make strategic choices between traditional, proven HR activities while experimenting with more innovative and progressive practices that fit the culture and structure of their organization. They must make these choices for and with their stakeholders and set beacons to improve the employee experience. In this chapter, we compare a broad range of activities on a *#ZigZagHR* continuum, balancing compliance and control of the traditional HR function with progressive HR practices that are more people-focused and based on trust.

The upside down pyramid

Paraphrasing a famous sociologist, Alex Inkeles, when defining a few decades ago, "What is Sociology?" he answered, "Sociology is what sociologists are doing."[108] It is quite appropriate to apply that today—HR is what HR professionals are doing!

Have you ever wondered what HR does on a day-to-day basis, whether these work activities are still relevant and how they have changed over time? The lifespan of companies has decreased from 67 to hardly 15 years. The half-life of knowledge is decreasing as well. Knowledge of today is obsolete tomorrow which means people must continuously learn to remain relevant and employable. This is the case for everyone—you too!

The different HR activities have traditionally been categorized by Patrick Wright and his colleagues (1998) as a pyramid with day-to-day "transactional HR" activities (benefits administration, record keeping and employee services) at the bottom of the pyramid taking up 65-75% of HR time; "traditional HR" activities (recruitment and selection, training, performance management, compensation, and employee relations) taking up 15-30% of HR time and "transformational HR" activities (knowledge management, strategic redirection and renewal, culture change, and management development) taking up 5-15% of HR time.[109]

In 2005, Dave Ulrich and Wayne Brockbank published the now HR classic entitled, *The HR Value Proposition*, a breakthrough in the development of strategic human resources. They asserted, more than a decade ago, HR transactional activities are no longer adding real value to the business.[110]

Yet, this does not mean that HR transactional activities are not important. On the contrary, they must be done at a level of excellence so as to avoid detracting from the employee—internal customer—experience. Imagine how an employee would react if their paycheck was not deposited in the bank on time, or their name was misspelled in your HR information system (HRIS), or you failed to enroll them in a particular benefit program.

This does, however, mean that HR must strive to turn the pyramid upside down. While we cannot ignore the traditional HR activities, HR should strive to make the transactional duties a smaller percentage of their daily efforts and spend more time focusing on the transformational activities. That's where the promise of IT augmentation comes in. While we argue that at the job level HR requires human intervention, at the HR task level (different parts of the job involving transactions) we can use non-humans (data, chatbots, algorithms, artificial intelligence, deep

Do you, as an HR practitioner, ask yourself if what you do day-in and day-out still has relevance?

learning, yes robots, etc.) to free up time for transactional and traditional activities and shift our efforts to transformational ones. HR can focus on the needs and experiences of the workforce and add real value to the business not just for today, but for long-term value. In this way, HR can make its value proposition come through.

Grinta of Chutzpah

Although not a mainstream English word, we enthusiastically propose the term *grinta* of Italian origin (*la forza di voluna*), loosely translated as the firmness of the will, meaning a determination to do or achieve something. It is synonymous with guts, determination, perseverance, and force of character. It totally describes what HR needs today: the courage to challenge the status quo; the perseverance to change our role—or even better—to take on the role of transformation architect; and having the character to grab our opportunities and embrace them with a can-do mentality.

We also think HR needs a dose of *chutzpa*: the arrogance, guts and impudence to rock the boat. In chapter 5 (*#ZigZagHR*-Careers) we described the need to adopt a growth mindset with an extreme dose of Pippi Longstocking arrogance: "I never have done it, so I think I can do it." Nobody can grasp the speed of technological developments or estimate what we will deal with a decade from now. That means we constantly need to do what we have never done before.

It's the end of HR as we know it (and I feel fine)

"It's the end of the world as we know it. That's great, it starts with an earthquake. Birds and snakes, and aeroplanes—And Lenny Bruce is not afraid…" Although there is no further link with the lyrics of this song, released by the American rockband REM in 1987, the song and its accompanying video clip describe pretty well HR's situation today—right in the middle of chaos.

Jacob Morgan, author of *The Employee Advantage* (2017), argues that "We need HR to not be HR."[111] With that, he means the momentum is opportune for HR to come to the foreground and evolve from a "hiring, firing and compliance" to a "moving the organization forward" mode. In a similar way, we are convinced that if HR wants to make a difference, it figuratively needs an earthquake to pry itself from the compliance and control mode where it somehow got stuck along the way.

As Jack Welch said, "People are just as important as finance." But unlike finance that has played the same role relatively speaking over the last 100 years, HR has been required

We also think that HR needs a dose of *chutzpa*: the arrogance, guts, and impudence to rock the boat.

to change significantly with very short intervals of about every two years. HR needs to think more like product development and IT than finance and search for ways to implement new technologies and practices to ensure continued company growth and success. IT/software development are always on the lookout for new technologies (Cloud versus Data Centers, agile versus waterfall project management, etc.). In the same way, HR must make significant changes to the way it operates to support the business. Innovative HR best and next practices spread at lightning speed through LinkedIn, "Disrupt HR" chapters around the world, Best Places to Work awards, international conferences, and webinars.

Innovation in HR: Where do we stand today?

During the past few years, a number of innovative HR trends have been introduced at a dazzling pace and magnitude, mainly in start-up companies who initially negated the value of the traditional HR function and did not have to bother with legacy systems.

Getting hard data and evidence-based knowledge as to the impact of these HR innovations on talent management, productivity, and employee satisfaction is much more difficult, although thought leader surveys on various progressive HR activities are showing that companies are increasingly adopting these innovative practices and experimenting. Here are some of these trends that are frequently mentioned:

- **CHANGING THE WORK ITSELF**—customizing the position for available talent, unbundling jobs when experienced (babyboomer) workers leave, getting away from job descriptions, not hiring for a specific job but for a set of competencies, and buying companies for acqui-hiring purposes.
- **FOCUSING ON THE WORK ENVIRONMENT**—focusing on challenging team-based work, a great and fun work atmosphere, diverse co-workers, overall relaxed company culture, and getting rid of job titles.
- **MANAGING EMPLOYEE LEARNING**—offering a wide range of learning modalities (collaborative, virtual, on-the-job learning, hybrid or blended), coaching, allowing people to work on personal projects, and increasing employability beyond the firm.
- **USING TALENT ACQUISITION TECHNOLOGIES**—using applicant tracking systems, artificial intelligence, social media, text-based sentiment analysis and gamification for recruitment, interviewing, selection, retirement savings, and internal employee communication.
- **PROVIDING CUSTOMIZED BENEFITS**—designing *à la carte* benefits, 13th month compensation, student loan payoff opportunities, supporting better tangible financial assets of employees over their lifetime, preparing people for longer and more resilient careers.

- **OFFERING LIFESTYLE PERKS**—making meal checks, free food and a variety of concierge services available from cleaning to shopping (let's not forget ironing the wash in Belgium).
- **PAYING ATTENTION TO WORK-LIFE INTEGRATION**—allowing paid time off, parental leave, and flexible work.
- **GIVING REAL-TIME FEEDBACK**—abolishing annual performance appraisals, implementing Objectives and Key Results (OKRs), requiring real-time feedback and coaching conversations, two-way mentoring, and real-time engagement.
- **HAVING FLEXIBLE WORK ARRANGEMENTS**—work anywhere any time, introducing "new working" schemes and making co-working spaces available.
- **INVESTING IN EMPLOYEE HEALTH AND LONGEVITY**—nudging employees to make good health and financial decisions, stress management, and an expanded definition of employer duty of care.
- **MAKING DATA-DRIVEN DECISIONS**—making use of people analytics, focusing on big data, exploring employee sentiment, and using predictive analytics.
- **FOCUSING ON WORKFORCE MANAGEMENT BEYOND EMPLOYEES**—expanding the definition of the workforce, co-employing employees, freelancers and contractors, new social contracts due to agile and gig-focused work, and even offering people cash to quit if there is no fit.

The above examples sound more applicable to the US than Europe because employment regulations and the social context are fundamentally different. It is our great interest to compare and contrast the idea of innovative HR practices between US and non-US countries (mainly Europe) and how these best practices are crossing the Atlantic in both directions. The following entrenched European HR practices (but innovative in the U.S.) have already influenced US HR and are likely to influence HR even more in the future.

- **PARENTAL LEAVE**—as the only developed country who does not provide government-mandated paid maternal, paternal, or parental leave for its employees, many US companies are taking this in their own hands and developing voluntary policies around this benefit that is of great interest to the millennial generation.
- **WORK-LIFE SEPARATION**—stop emails on weekends, evenings, statutory vacations, and holidays unless there is an emergency.
- **GENEROUS BENEFITS**—such as annual paid vacation, meal checks, and gas/petrol cards for commuters.

This brings up an interesting question that we leave open for further discussion: which country has the most innovative HR practices? If so, which organizations, industries or sector?

#ZigZagHR-Operations does not advocate complete *tabula rasa* in HR—since this would throw out the good with the bad. Instead, *#ZigZagHR*-Operations allows us to automate or augment transactional activities with IT (e-HRM) and reconcile proven traditional HR practices with transformational activities that are innovative and progressive and fit the newer context of the world of work and the worker. It also allows HR to make operational choices related to evolving HR activities and experiments—see what works and does not work in organizations in terms of people management practices.

> **#ZigZagHR is aimed at making sound operational choices on the traditional-progressive continuum from extreme traditional to radical innovative HR practices.**

Ultimately, it is a way to shape HR, befitting the new reality of the fourth industrial and improving HR value to all stakeholders.

Choosing is (not) losing

Move over André Gide. *Choisir, c'est renoncer* (choosing is losing) is less applicable in HR today. It is a strategic imperative of HR to make choices that improve the talent position of an organization.

In Beyond HR, Boudreau and Ramstad (2007) define "talentship" as building organizational effectiveness by improving decisions that affect or depend on human capital where they make the biggest strategic difference. In making these choices, HR programs must consider three anchor points:[112]

- **EFFICIENCY**—how investments affect programs and practices
- **EFFECTIVENESS**—how programs and practices affect talent and organizational pools
- **IMPACT**—how talent and organization pools affect sustainable strategic success

Let's illustrate making these operational choices HR faces with 10 examples of *#ZigZagHR*-Operations in different HR functional areas that are receiving great attention today by employers and employees alike in the work place (see figure 3).[113]

FIGURE 3. A Continuum of *#ZigZagHR*-Activities

Traditional HR		Progressive HR
Annual Performance Appraisal	*Performance Management* ⟷	No Performance Appraisal
Paid Time Off Based on Seniority	*Paid Time Off* ⟷	Unlimited Paid Time Off
Fixed Working Hours	*Work Flexibility* ⟷	Flexible Working Hours
Confidental Pay	*Salary Transparency* ⟷	Transparent Pay
Limited Employee Value Proposition	*Employer Branding* ⟷	Strong Employee Value Proposition
Process Centric	*Engagement* ⟷	Employee Centric
Diversity & Inclusion	*Diversity* ⟷	DIBS
Recruitment	*Talent Management* ⟷	Retention
Control	*Organizational Culture* ⟷	Trust
HR Audit	*Value Measurement* ⟷	Disruptive Audit

#ZIGZAGHR—WHO WILL MISS THE ANNUAL PERFORMANCE REVIEW?

#ZigZagHR: Do I continue to have annual performance appraisals or replace it with a customized set of coaching and developmental practices?

In traditional companies, performance management systems culminated in a key event, namely the annual performance appraisal meeting conducted between the manager and the direct report supported by multi-rater input with some form of 360 degree evaluation. The performance appraisal session—loathed by both manager "rater" and employee "ratee"—was used to identify areas of employee development, allocating rewards (merit increases), documenting possible disciplinary action, and some form of self-expression of employee wants and needs. The many pitfalls of this type of "rank and yank" performance appraisals and the cost associated with them have been widely documented. The trend of abolishing performance appraisals (not performance management) has taken root in many US companies since 2015 and is now close to being considered a mainstream practice as a large number of companies have followed suit.[114]

The most interesting finding in this trend is that when reinventing their performance management systems, companies are realizing a one-size-fits-all approach no longer works and they need to customize their performance management practices to fit their own organizational culture. In *The New Global Performance Paradigm: Reinventing Performance Reviews*, Lisbeth Claus and Scott Baker (2015) report that in this reinvention process, companies have instituted a number of practices that usually include one or more of the following features: developing objectives and key results (OKRs) with all employees, providing immediate real-time employee feedback, engaging in coaching through regular coaching conversations, focusing on strengths management, and taking advantage of teachable moments as they occur.[115]

Please note: *#ZigZagging* is not without any challenges. Companies abolishing performance appraisals struggle with how to decouple merit-based pay—traditionally based on the outcome of the annual performance appraisals—from the review, how to fill the gaping coaching skill gap of most managers, how to identify high-performers in an unbiased manner, and last, but not least, what performance indicators to document or not?

#ZIGZAGHR—LONG LIVE THE HOLIDAYS!

#ZigZagHR: Is an accrual-based system of paid time off used or do employees have unlimited vacation time?

Should companies use a traditional "earned or accrual-based" time off system based on years of tenure or a more progressive formula, unlimited paid time off (UPTO). This progressive HR practice is developing rapidly in the US employment framework due to a lack of statutory protection of employees when it comes to taking time off. Compared to Europeans, American employees have no statutory vacation days or holidays—the only industrialized country not to provide that benefit! It is striking that the American workforce is also not very good at taking time off from work and they often leave unused vacation days on the table each year (an average of 4.9 days). Some companies even allow them to accrue unused days.[116] Although there are many pros and cons to instituting UPTO, it is very popular as a benefit with US start-up companies, especially to attract and retain the millennial generation.

#ZIGZAGHR—TOGETHER IN A COMMUTER TRAFFIC JAM

#ZigZagHR: Should work be structured around fixed time and location constraints, or can employees just work anytime from anywhere?

For many employees, work still consists of commuting from home to work to show up at a certain workplace and be engaged in the office during a certain proverbial "9 to 5" work time with allocated breaks. For many workers, there is very little flexibility, even: during rush hour, when public transportation is not available, or during a strike, or during extreme weather conditions, or for when a doctor's visit is required during work time. While the physical presence at increasingly open office workspaces allows for greater collaborative work, it also distracts workers from much needed concentration. While open workspaces are hailed the promise of better collaboration (and cheaper office space), it often leads to a lack of concentration, productivity, and general well being.

Yet today, the widespread availability of information and communication technology (ICT) allows knowledge workers to pretty much work anytime from anywhere. Flexible work—known by many other names and variations such as telecommunuting, telework, flextime, remote work, co-working spaces, compressed workdays, and other flexible work arrangements, also coined "new working"—is not only rapidly growing, but is now becoming mainstream in many global companies. Statistics about remote and flexible work from Global Workplace Analytics show in 2017 half of the US workforce holds a job that is compatible with at least partial telework and that 20-25% of the US workforce teleworks at some frequency.[117] Fortune 1000 companies—the ranking of companies in the U.S. based on annual revenue and established published by *Fortune Magazine*—are entirely revamping their workspace around the fact that employees are already mobile and not at their desks 50-60% of the time.[118] This has also engendered the growth and popularity of co-working spaces, where remote workers come into the office occasionally and use a rolling desk or rent a hot desk from a third party to mingle with workers from other companies. Although several years ago, companies like IBM, and later Yahoo, pioneered a path allowing employees to work remotely, they have reversed some of their remote work policies requiring their employees to work at company offices or shared spaces. Their employees are again required to show up at work—whether a fixed or satellite office—in spite of the fact they have the most advanced technologies.[119]

In his 2016 doctoral dissertation, *The Distance Dilemma*, Nick Van Der Meulen (Rotterdam School of Management, Erasmus University, and researcher at MIT Sloan School of Management) investigates the effect of flexible working practices on performance in the digital workspace.[120] He describes the distance dilemma in flexible work as the trade-off between opportunities for concentration (at home) and collaboration (at the office). Van der Meulen also investigates the impact of temporal and physical separation from others such as work colleagues, and customers on individual workers, managers, and the organization. While remote work stimulates a worker's focus through reduced distractions, it may frustrate interdependent collaborative work through reduced presence and social capital.

According to the author, a different management style is needed to overcome the pitfalls of remote work because managers are no longer able to observe employees at work and give up control through the lack of visibility. Managers should not keep their eye on the clock but shift their focus on the work itself and ultimately, the results. Transparency, communication and a coaching leadership style are the key success factors of this form of "new" remote work. It is important to mention that this openness and accessibility must be supported by an "any time, any place" communication technology.

In spite of these limitations, flexible and remote are options that should not immediately be dismissed by HR, but rather be on their radar screen and seriously taken under consideration as it is an inevitable form of work in the future—if not already today—for many progressive companies. Introducing work done anytime and anywhere requires an organizational capability that is closely linked to the corporate culture and leadership style of the employer. While it is increasingly embraced by many US companies and even has strong legislative and cultural support in the Netherlands, it is still in its infancy in Belgium and many other countries.

This presents another dilemma between the necessity to, on one hand, quickly adapt to the new economic and social reality and, on the other hand, the understandable caution not to destroy this form of new work that has evolved as a result of social and emancipatory motives. In the U.S., remote and flexible work—whether as employee or freelancers—are becoming the norm when recruiting knowledge workers, especially millennials. This demands a totally different management approach for teams, their leaders, and HR in onboarding and socializing new recruits in the culture of the organization.

#ZIGZAGHR—SHOW ME THE MONEY!

#ZigZagHR: Should salary information be kept confidential or transparent to all?

Are salaries confidential information known only to a few in the organization (HR, finance and executives) or disclosed and fully transparent to all? Proponents of salary transparency use economic and inequality arguments to argue that sunlight on employee salaries is the best disinfectant. The inequality argument is that salary transparency brings pay gaps in the open and shines light on continued gender and other discriminatory pay practices. The economic argument for pay transparency is based on improved market efficiency. Defenders of salary confidentiality use morale, productivity, and privacy arguments to show negative effects of open salary disclosure. The morale argument—invoking the equity theory of motivation—suggests it is demoralizing when people find out they earn less than their peers based on input— whether due to pay inequities or salary compression—and that it may affect job satisfaction. The privacy argument goes further than disclosure of personal information and argues that it allows for better negotiation—whether the balance tips in favor of the employer or the savvy employee. Complicating the salary disclosure debate is that in knowledge work, it is much more difficult to accurately measure the relationship between pay and productivity than in the traditional widget-producing manufacturing economy.[121]

Norway and Sweden have passed pay transparency laws and are currently studying its impact. Pay transparency in the U.S. is not common with the exception of jobs in government-related institutions and for the C-suite of public companies. The popularity of websites such as "Glassdoor.com" is rapidly changing the salary sunshine debate. Being a true "employer of choice," not by self-identification and market signaling but through the experience of real people inside the company, is paramount.

Although base salary is only one component of the total compensation package with record low unemployment and skill shortages, pay transparency is becoming more and more important to workers. Companies are doing everything to attract and retain their talent. If they are accused of not being fair in paying their employees, or paying different rates based on gender, race, etc., they will immediately be less attractive to the best talent. Such pay gaps and other salary inequities affects employer branding—which brings us to the next #ZigZagHR-Practice.

#ZIGZAGHR—EMPLOYER BRANDING: WHERE HR MEETS MARKETING!

#ZigZagHR: Is your "employee value proposition" (EVP) a marketing artifact or a true lived experience by employees?

In *The War for Talent*, Michaels, Handfield-Jones, and Axelrod (2001) develop the concept of employer branding. In order to effectively attract, develop and retain the best talent, organizations focus heavily on creative HR practices. This is done through signaling an attractive EVP to the potential market of employees and the use of employment branding before, during and after employment. By focusing on an EVP (Why should I come and work for you?), companies attract the best talent because they are "the best place to work." According to the authors, there are four basic brand propositions that attract high-performing employees:[122]

1. **GO WITH THE WINNER**—employees are most interested in growth and advancement
2. **BIG RISK, BIG REWARDS**—employees value advancement and compensation
3. **SAVE THE WORLD**—employees need an inspiring mission
4. **LIFESTYLE**—employees seek flexibility and a good fit with the boss

Today, most employers use employer branding and "employer of choice" labels as an integral part of their talent management strategy. But the fundamental question remains, is the EVP of the company real or not? In other words, does the narrative of what it is like to work at that company fit the actual employee experience? The reasons why employees join a company are not the same as the reasons why they stay at a company. So, while employers may have a fantastic value proposition to attract people, they may falter at keeping them because the experience does not live up to the expectations. How do managers reconcile the "war on talent" with the "war on retention of talent?" The activities related to the acquisition of high-performing talent are very different from the ability to engage and retain talent once they are onboard. This is where the employee experience comes in—a concept we already mentioned in previous chapters.

Many companies are implementing an Employee Net Promoter Score (e-NPS), similar to what companies use for measuring the customer experience. The NPS for a Customer Experience at an airline: "Would you recommend KLM as an airline to a friend or family member?" For HR, the e-NPS: "Would you recommend KLM as a place to work to a friend or family member?" Progressive companies track this score monthly by company, department, and manager.[123]

#ZIGZAGHR—FROM PROCESS-CENTRIC TO EMPLOYEE-CENTRIC

#ZigZagHR: Can true engagement happen without focusing on the employee experience?

Jacob Morgan in *The Employee Experience* (2017) shows that a hallmark of the 3rd industrial revolution era is that employers focus their employee relations efforts on employee engagement.[124] The idea was that making employees happy was important and that happiness would engage them so that they could perform better and be more productive. A whole industry flourished around measuring the work engagement of employees with their employer.

> **In spite of many efforts to engage employees and conduct annual engagement surveys, these surveys show a high proportion of the workforce around the world remains highly disengaged and many employees are only moderately engaged.**

According to a 2018 Gallup report, only 15 percent of employees are engaged in their daily work globally and 33 percent nationally (U.S.).[125] As a result of these failed efforts and the advent of the 4th industrial revolution, many employers are now focusing on the employee experience and improving the various touchpoints that employees have with management, HR, and the company. To get real-time feedback on what stands in the way of employee engagement, many companies are abandoning the annual engagement surveys for regular employee pulse surveys to understand the employee sentiment on a day-to-day or weekly basis. Getting the pulse on any given day or workweek of "How are you feeling toward [an aspect of] the company?" allows companies to measure how different employee personas feel in the moment and respond immediately to what deters employees from bringing their fullest self to the job. While challenges remain, employee pulse or sentiment surveys have many advantages over period engagement surveys.

- **MORE TIMELY FEEDBACK**—what is important today rather than during the past year?
- **ABILITY TO MODIFY OR EMPHASIZE CERTAIN TIMELY TOPICS WITH EMPLOYEES**—how is the flu epidemic or planned public transportation strike affecting our work?
- **IDENTIFY KEY TRENDS AND UNDERSTAND DIFFERENCES**—based on function, department, location, tenure, etc., and how is an issue affecting employees differently?

- **MAKE IMMEDIATE COURSE CORRECTIONS**—change course by one or two degrees rather than make a 10 to 20 degree correction when the problem has escalated.
- **WORK IN A MORE AGILE MANNER**—this is especially the case in high-tech organization or those working in an agile management environment that may dictate frequent shifting of resources as employees are likely to have different teams and managers.
- **ABILITY TO ADAPT LEADERSHIP STYLE AND PRACTICE CONTINGENCY MANAGEMENT**—provides leaders and coaches with timely feedback to adjust their style immediately based on the situation.

However, there are a number of challenges to make effective use of pulse surveys:

- **CULTURAL DIFFERENCES**—power distance or hierarchy may focus the content more or less on the employee-manager relationship versus the overall cultural climate of the organization.
- **THE IMPACT OF NEGATIVE EVENTS**—local layoffs or tenuous labor relations may have a greater impact over a long period of time that the pulse survey may easily miss.
- **PULSE SURVEY RESULTS**—how do pulse survey results in different locations affect management decisions (e.g., investment of resources, hiring decisions, etc.) when in fact they may be based on cultural differences?

These sentiment gauges allow organizations to identify where manager have and can improve, curate knowledge into learning content, and design new people management processes that not only improve the employee experience, but also engages different employee personas at the level they want to be engaged. David Green and Laura Stevens describe how this marketing phenomenon of "continuous listening" also needs to be used by HR as part of people analytics. Such ongoing listening is not just another app or software to take the employee's pulse, it is a way to evolve in a quick and agile way from a soft and process-oriented way of working to an HR function that is evidence-based and employee centric.[126]

#ZIGZAGHR—DIBS—THE NEW BUZZWORD?
#ZigZagHR: Diversity and inclusion or intersectionality and authenticity?

According to the Society of Human Resource Management (2016), diversity relates to who we bring into the organization while inclusion is how we make people feel welcome when they are here.[127] Diversity has finally moved from a focus on race and gender (its US historical roots in the civil rights and women's social movements) to a broader focus on global cultural diversity. It now encompasses many elements including both person-based traits as well as a host of ascribed and achieved social characteristics. But having a diverse workforce or legal compliance with anti-discrimination laws does not necessarily make everyone feel welcome. That's where inclusion comes in and how comfortable different people are and how well they are accepted by others in the workplace.

Diversity and inclusion are now viewed as an imperative by (external) customers and (internal) employees alike. It is not only widely believed, but also shown through a growing body of research that diversity and inclusion impact overall organizational performance in terms of brand, purpose, and team-based performance. It is generally believed people can do their best work when there is a critical mass of people (some different and some similar to them) in the workplace to interact with and the place is inclusive. While diversity in the workplace is far from being achieved, HR departments now have functional activities directly related to promoting workplace diversity and inclusion. Yet, in everyday HR operations, diversity still focuses on pigeonholing a person based on a few usually observable characteristics. Some examples might be: you are a university-educated young man born in Belgium from Moroccan Muslim parents; you are a single mother who is also a working professional; you are an older worker or a millennial; you are covered in body tattoos!

In spite of all the diversity and inclusion efforts, many organizations still have a long way to go. When looking at the diversity profile of the workforce—or still the lack thereof—think of the different gaps and ceilings in employment opportunities, pay and other equal opportunities by gender, race, and differentially abled people that currently exist in the workforce. Despite the attention of companies and the allocation of many resources, IT companies, for example, have not been able to truly diversify their workforce. It could be argued that HR has basically not provided real return of value in this arena. One of the proofs that's often put forward is whether a random sample of a company's customers would match a random sample of their employees without one being able to distinguish between them.

A new and more empowered paradigm has emerged, driven largely by the millennial generation who grew up with more diverse and team-based education and exposure. Etymologically, the notion of inclusion—being included within a group—has a connotation that the person who is different has to step up and become part of the dominant group and take on some of those expected behaviors. Even if "diverse" people get into these organization, they may not reveal their true self, thrive, or want to be there and feel included.

A more progressive diversity concept is intersectionality. The term intersectionality, coined as early as 1989 by legal scholar Kimberlé Crenshaw, refers to the multiple dimensions of a person's social identity and how they relate either to systems and structures of discrimination or forms of privilege. Its application in the workplace is more recent. Intersectionality is the idea that multiple group identities intersect to create a whole that is different from the component identities.[128]

Laws and policies usually only address one form of marginalized identity. The "intersectionality wheel" is a commonly used graphic representation of these different social identities: a broad mosaic of different factors—as many as 50 personal and social characteristics—make up an identity. This approach allows people to bring their own authenticity into the workplace—some of which may not fit the mold of the observable, diverse characteristics.[129]

In line with the notion of intersectionality, Andrew Solomon, in *Far from the Tree* (2012) explores the concept of "vertical" (or directly inherited) and "horizontal" (or independently divergent) identities. Examples of horizontal identities are differently abled people who do not share the values and preferences with their progenitors, such as deafness, dwarfism, Down syndrome, autism, schizophrenia, multiple severe disabilities, prodigies, transgender individuals, etc.[130] How do they become full-fledge contributors to society and secure gainful employment? Many people who do not "fit" in have a hard time getting their foot in the door through the interview and selection process because we carry unconscious and conscious biases and stereotypes as to who fits in! How can employers tap into part of the skills set that we need and employ people who have the needed skills, but perhaps lack some other conventional skill? Neurodiverse people who have the knowledge, skills, and work ethic, but perhaps lack social skills;[131] tattooed people who don't have the acceptable "look;" ethnically diverse people who belong to more than one minority group.[132]

> **In progressive companies, D&I (Diversity and Inclusion) is being replaced by DIBS (Diversity, Inclusion, Belonging, & Support).**

HR must pay greater attention to identify which parts of the interview and selection process needs to change to make people with different identities part of the workforce. HR's attention should not stop with selection processes, but continue with onboarding and appropriate training. This encourages everyone to bring their true self to work and not feel excluded.

Perhaps we should be inspired by some examples of American universities that include a trained recruiting expert (search advocate) to enhance the equity, validity, and diversity of search and selection efforts. Search advocates are trained on current research, theory and practical strategies to help search committees test their thinking, address complex process concerns, improve search validity and equity, understand and promote diversity, mitigate conflicts of interest, and anticipate and address a variety of other potential bias risks.[133]

While not perfect, HR has made more advancement with diversity and inclusion in the past 10 years—simply powered by the naturally highly competitive environment for people and their expectations—than all the laws and D&I programs or initiatives combined! Millenials are more alert to diversity and equal opportunities and, compared to other generations, are speaking up and do not tolerate exclusion, discrimination, and intolerance. Companies are so desperate to hire and retain great employees. The competitive labor market and shortage of skilled workers is becoming the driving force for a smooth transition to an inclusive workplace. For those companies who do not, they will soon fail as the new generation of employees will vote with their feet and work for other companies. Compared to 10 years ago, the HR response today is more "what can we do" versus "here's what we can't do."

The issue of diversity and inclusion in other countries around the world may be more complex than in the U.S., which has a longer legal and cultural tradition in this arena. How does a Caucasian Christian woman in the Middle-East, a Sudanese woman in Europe, or a black person working in China or Germany get hired across all levels of the organization and feel included?

#ZIGZAGHR—IS TALENT MANAGEMENT PASSÉ?
ZigZagHR: Are we in a "war for talent" or in a "war on retention" mode?

In the past two decades, organizations realized that in spite of economic cycles, there was an ever-present shortage of the right talent in terms of competencies and willingness to fully engage in work. In order to have a fit-for-future workforce, the "war for talent" led to the development of talent management. In talent management, the strategic choices and operational functional HR activities are geared towards achieving a competitive advantage through people.

With an increasingly competitive global talent market for the right talent, HR's emphasis was focused on talent acquisition and onboarding as its table stakes. Obviously with the aging of the workforce, globalization, and the growth of the IT sector, the ever increasing need for finding a competent workforce and attracting the best are ever present. Yet, very few employers focus on developing and managing their employees with the same effort they dedicate to acquiring them.

With the growing appeal of the gig economy, the allure of self employment and entrepreneurship, the weakening social contract between employers and employees, and concerns for work-life integration of a generation of people who may have to work much longer, getting the talent on board is only part of the equation. The war for talent suggests that company A hires a top-notch employee from company B and company

B hires a top-notch employee from company A—a lose-lose situation. Current talent management has moved beyond this and the battle now is about how to engage and retain valuable employees by offering them compelling experiences at work.

#ZIGZAGHR—FROM COMMAND AND CONTROL TOWARDS A CULTURE OF TRUST

#ZigZagHR: Do we use a trust-but-verify or a trust-and-let-go approach in our day-to-day work?

HR is charged with compliance of employment laws, statutes, and regulatory requirements such as reporting, disclosure, posting, retention and maintenance of employee files, employment contracts, a variety of benefit plan reporting and disclosures, and more broadly the legal requirements in the treatment of the workforce on a wide range of issues. As a result, they not only develop a number of compliance tools—such as employee handbooks, job descriptions, HR policies and procedures, workplace safety manuals, compliance posters, etc.—but they have geared their control system on the compliance role. It goes without saying that it is not wise for an employer to ignore HR compliance. Yet, it is becoming more and challenging as there are more laws and regulations on diverse employment subjects, it is highly complex and changing and the workforce is more informed of their rights and becoming more eager to engage in a law suit. Hence, the control function of HR to ensure compliance is growing and often one of the reasons why HR is often viewed as a bogeyman, largely regarded as an object of fear, inflexibility, and control who frighten people into good behavior.

In many progressive workplaces, the focus is shifting away from control to a more people-oriented trust role by moving from the "trust and verify" (a somewhat untrustworthy political phrase) to "trust and let go" (assume your employees will do the right thing). The HR rule book is slowly being replaced by a manifesto of how to treat people we work with and what we expect from them.

Nan S. Russells, who focuses on trust in the workplace, provides a simple *#ZigZag-Answer* on the control versus let go dilemma: "When outcome is essential and matters more than the relationship, use trust, but verify. When relationship matters more than any single outcome, don't use it."[134] The operational choice does not solely depend on the culture or leadership style that an organization espouses or whether they espouse McGregor's motivation theory X—people cannot be trusted, but must be coerced and/or controlled as they have little ambition and will not seek responsibility—or theory Y— work is an important part of people's life, they are capable and want to make a difference.[135] The choice of control versus let go also depends on the nature of the work and the structure of the organization. In highly regulated industries, in life or death situations, in cases of safety and security, there should be trust, but make sure to verify. In other situations, go with trust first and build trusted relationships.[136]

In today's progressive workplaces, HR is not forced into the role of policing. The pendulum is definitely swinging toward trusting that people will do the right thing rather than controlling for the few "bad apples" that may force the policing of work practices.

> **HR still must fulfill its control and compliance function and may have a hard time letting go! The challenge for *#ZigZagHR* is to create employee and labor relations that use the best traditional methods of compliance with innovative methods of trust. No other place in HR today is *#ZigZagging* more importantly than here!**

How does HR balance the need for control and compliance with attaining the desired outcome by letting go to build effective a culture of real trust, teamwork, and leadership?

#ZIGZAGHR—HOW DO WE MEASURE HR VALUE
 # ZigZagHR: HR audit or disruptive audit?

A traditional best practice for HR organization is to conduct a regular HR audit and take a more objective look at HR practices and their effectiveness.

Yet, with the current changes HR is experiencing, it is questionable whether an HR audit is sufficient to respond to the changing environment or we need a more disruptive audit to radically transform HR.

An HR audit looks objectively at the organization's HR policies, practices, procedures, and strategies to evaluate whether HR practices are adequate, legal, and effective. The goal of an HR audit is to protect the organization, establish best practices and identify opportunities for improvement. While HR audits are a way to see whether the systems are in place to achieve operational excellence, they tend to be driven by functional experts and the need to control and reduce risk.

In Peter Hinssen's book, *The Day after Tomorrow* (2017), he proposes the idea of a "disruptive audit" where multi-disciplinary teams with diverse profiles and a passion for innovation and change challenge the status quo, drive the company outside of the comfort zone, question everything, look at things from different angles, rip apart, put back together, experiment, and challenge the status quo.[137] Rather than viewing their activities from their own process perspective, HR should view it from the customer's perspective, i.e., the employee, the manager they serve.

Make *#ZigZagHR*-decisions

How do we know in HR whether we make a good operational decision or not? How do we know which innovation is the right one for our organization and whether these progressive practices will work or not? Are we, as HR leaders, more attuned to the desires and expectations of employees, or more concerned with business needs or our own processes? Do we make short-term decisions for today or sustainable choices for the future?

Here are a few *#ZigZagHR* practices that we have observed.

PARTNER STRATEGICALLY WITH THE BUSINESS: #BUSINESS ACUMEN

One of the best ways for HR to strategically partner with the business is, first of all, to get to know the business—whether for-profit or not. From his experience as a manager and team leader working with talented people, Denny Long, in his book *Managing Genius* (2015), explains what it really means to know the business and how essential it is to have this knowledge to manage people successfully. He lists eight important knowledge areas that integrate with one another to get a wholistic view of the business that HR work supports.[138]

- Organizational chart
- Key players
- Customers
- Lingo and business speak
- How things work
- Supply chain
- Cost of doing business
- Technology

In a strategic relationship with the executive team and management, HR is working on the future and translates the strategic goals of the organization to concrete HR strategies, priorities and operational plans. HR has an understanding of the priorities, good business, and financial acumen and their pulse is constantly on how the market is evolving. This knowledge reaches much further than the HR domain-specific body of knowledge and is necessary so that the ideal workforce combination can be recruited, selected, developed, managed, and retained.

AUGMENT HR WITH TECHNOLOGY: #THERE_IS_AN_APP_FOR_THAT

Many different software applications have been developed around some of the HR progressive practices that we have illustrated. These apps assist with facilitating and documenting employee feedback, coaching, teamwork, tracking, communication, and other experiences by collecting ambient and self-reported data that allows the organization to identify bottlenecks in the employee-manager touchpoints, curate knowledge for learning content, and respond with real time data-driven decisions. Many tools—from simple process automation to artificial intelligence—are now being used in HR to search for passive candidates, analyze CVs and application forms, track applicants, book interviews, conduct and code interviews, answer HR questions via chatbots, and more.[139] These apps do not only allow for the automation of many routine HR practices, they also make it possible to better know the worker as an internal customer and avoid unconscious biases in HR decisions.

With increased automation and artificial intelligence, the people value comes from the culture of the organization and how well people work with other people—whether on their teams or with customers. The time for copycat HR operations is over! HR becomes the architect of the workforce experience.

FOCUS ON THE HR TRIPLE BOTTOM LINE FOR SUSTAINABLE SUCCESS

HR's role is to provide the transactional activities at the A-level of excellence so the employee experience with the touchpoints of the organization are flawless and seamless. In that endeavor, HR must focus on adding value to the HR triple bottom line: the customer, the business, and the workforce and balancing their different needs and experiences. That's where the sweet spot lies, namely what is good for the worker is also good for the company and its customers.

HR must focus on adding value
to the HR triple bottom line:
the customer, the business,
and the workforce and balancing
their different needs and
experiences.

STIMULATE SOCIAL ACTIVISM

While in the past, corporations have been lobbying for their self-interest in terms of lower taxes, and less regulations while labor unions have focused on the bread and butter issues of their members. Society is now looking at employers to play a larger role in solving some of society's social problems that affect work and the workers—whether it is sexual harassment, transgender and gay rights, healthcare, immigration, racism, mental health, or basic income. While HR cannot alone solve all these problems, they must encourage their companies to play a greater role in the societal debate.

Two specific examples come to mind with regard to women in the IT sector and sexual harassment in the U.S. workplace (likely a wordwide phenomenon that is about to be brought in the open everywhere). We have witnessed the explosion of sexual harassment scandals in the U.S. workplace and the unacceptable behavior that has been allowed to continue in many organizations despite so-called complaints to HR and independent investigations that were conducted. We keep on witnessing the lack of women in the technology sector or on corporate boards due to the conscious bias in selection despite the so-called efforts of IT companies to court and attract them and laws requiring quotas of female board representation.

 "Where was HR?" It is almost impossible not to think about Uber while writing this. Not so long ago, they had a work environment that was pervasive with sexual harassment and misconduct. HR was part of the problem in that the culture continued. The lack of courage and inaction of HR resulted in a talented founder CEO losing his job and a declining value of the company. The company situation showed very poorly on the new dynamic, innovative, and progressive HR practices when we think about a young start-up on the Pacific West Coast of the United States.

How do we as an HR profession stand up for inappropriate culture and practices? Being a business partner should not mean that we look the other way or condone unacceptable people practices for the sake of profit or other goals.

It should be clear by now that we favor *#ZigZagHR*-Operations. Changing HR one step and one activity at a time leads to change that ranges from small to radical improvements of the total employee experience.

#*ZIGZAGHR*-LEADING PRACTICES

- Partner strategically with the business
- Augment HR with technology
- Focus on the HR triple bottom line for sustainable success
- Stimulate social activism

Traditional firms tend to rely on tangible assets and are lagging in pay, profit, growth and productivity. Progressive firms rely mainly on intangible assets and use talent, data, and computer power as their new means of production.

Double check your *#ZigZagHR* decisions and ask yourself the following questions:[140]

- Is the decision **ETHICAL**?
- Is the decision **FAIR** to employees?
- Is the decision **GREEN** in terms of the carbon footprint?
- Is the decision-making process **TRANSPARENT** and open for scrutiny?
- Is the decision **SUSTAINABLE** in the long run?

■ **And, it starts with you!**

IN SUMMARY

In *#ZigZagHR*-Operations, we juxtapose a variety of HR activities that are rapidly evolving from more traditional HR practices—which tend to be compliance and control oriented—to more progressive ones that appear more innovative, employee-centric and trust-based. The operational choices that HR makes are not limited to its functional activities, but must also include the augmentation of its transactional activities with IT and e-HRM applications. In the newer context of the world of work and the worker, HR must balance the needs of its various stakeholders and find the triple bottom line sweet spot between external customers, business, and workforce requirements.

7

#ZigZagHR Ecosystem

NO (WO)MAN IS AN ISLAND

7

The dynamics described in the previous chapters could signal a golden era for HR. To survive, HR must be more innovative, creative, agile, transparent, and strategically *#ZigZag* between traditional and progressive HR practices. How do we go beyond the buzzwords, books, and blogposts that are far away from day-to-day reality in our own company? Not by throwing our practices overboard! We can't emphasize enough that *#ZigZagHR* is not a plea for tabula rasa. *#ZigZagHR* is a plea to reinvent ourselves, to *#ZigZag* strategically, to use the innovative "three-box" model of Vijay Govindarajan and Chris Trimble, and to apply it to HR in our own context. The vision can (and must) be bold, but the steps toward it are small and manageable. It is also important for HR to know what happens in the world outside of their own organization, to scan the environment, and determine what impact new developments can and will have on HR, on your company, and all its stakeholders. In this chapter, we delve more into the importance of innovation, the three-box model, and describe how HR can apply this model to itself. In addition, we call on HR leaders to join our *#ZigZagHR*-Ecosystem and develop solutions together that benefit all stakeholders and that no single stakeholder could realize alone.

Innovation is key!

#ZigZagHR is, in the first place, a call to innovate. These innovations can be small incremental and linear but they must be aimed at optimizing the current delivery of HR services and make our practices more worker-friendly while being efficient, effective and impactful. Of course, we also must have radical non-linear innovations where we challenge the status quo and we completely redefine the value HR adds to its stakeholders. In his book *The Day after Tomorrow*, Peter Hinssen proposes a sublime model of innovation where he focuses on the attention, time, resources, talent, and energy that needs to be invested to be innovative. According to Hinssen, we should devote 70% of our time to today, 20% to tomorrow and 10% to *the day after tomorrow* in our organizations.[141] Everyone in the organization should be aware that it is important to concern ourselves with the day after tomorrow, because that's where the value creation—at least in the long term—lies. But, at the same time, every organization also realizes that in the day-to-day work reality, we barely have enough spare time, resources, talent, or energy to invest in the future. This also is true for what we do in HR.

Until World War II, the dominant paradigm for most companies was closed innovation: innovations were jealously kept secret and outside information was generally not sought or integrated. The drivers behind this logic have, in the meantime, (happily) disappeared, together with the not-invented-here syndrome, where only innovations that are developed inside the walls of the enterprise are considered good and trustworthy.

> **Today progressive companies—how big and successful they are—understand that valuable knowledge resides outside of their walls.**

In open innovation external and internal sources are combined, whether in the development or the marketing of new products and services. Open innovation, propagated by Henry Chesbrough, professor and executive director of the Center for Open Innovation at UC Berkeley, is related to user innovation. Companies like IBM and P&G were early adopters of that.[142]

Building an ecosystem as an answer to innovation

Today, organizations are more and more attacked and disrupted from unexpected corners; therefore, they are always on a mission, looking for the silver bullet or the secret ingredient to be truly innovative. To get there, they go through predictable phases, often without sustainable success: attracting employees who were innovative somewhere else or were involved in a successful start-up, making sure that leadership behaves like VCs (venture capitalists), and even setting up an innovation board. However, this rarely succeeds as organizations behave as organisms or as giant animals with ears and eyes, a mouth, a stomach, and a tail.

Many organizations still function as a closed mechanism: people don't go out for lunch or meetings. It is easier and more practical and effective for the employer to offer everything internally: from food to yoga and training in house. This is understandable from a pure budgetary perspective. However, this also means that the face-to-face network is limited to the colleagues who work together in the workplace. That means not only that knowledge sharing is not internally stimulated, but also that little or no new knowledge, information and oxygen enters the company from the outside. This is also bad for the worker's personal life—because when employees lose their job they also, to a large extent, lose their social network. Closed organizations tend to be slow to react and are generally not agile enough to change.

> The world outside the walls of the company is constantly developing and evolving while the DNA of closed companies remains unchanged and they keep approaching the same problems in the same way, often with more effort and less people. In vain, of course!

Jack Welch once said: "If the rate of change on the outside exceeds the rate of change on the inside, the end is near." That sound perhaps a bit melodramatic, but Jack may be right—or not?

An ecosystem has no boundaries and limits. It constantly adapts, moves and grows. It absorbs new knowledge and information, reacts and transforms itself. It is the interaction with all other actors that creates the added value of the total ecosystem. Organizations who do that have an ecosystem mindset that is so typical of start-up companies.

No (wo)man is an island

The notion of an ecosystem was introduced in 1935 by the English botanist Arthur Tansley and later further developed by the American ecologist Eugene Odum. It consists of two mutually influencing components: the living community and the biotope.[143] An ecosystem can be viewed as a community of living organisms that interact with each other and their environment, and collectively, continuously adapt to external disruptions by developing and sharing resources. While both Arthur and Eugene did not link their work with management (or for that matter *#ZigZagHR*), there are many similarities between nature as an ecosystem and organizations who function as an ecosystem.

Typical for an ecosystem is its resilience and ability to be self healing. The more diverse the organisms are in this living community and their interactions, the more resilient nature is. This also holds true for organizations and for HR. Just as in nature, resilience has its limits and in the same manner that a complete ecosystem can be irreparably or even totally destroyed, so too the resilience of organizations, individuals, and HR has its limits.

We can learn a lot from nature in terms of innovation as ultimately, nature had millions of years time to come up with the best solutions for the most challenging problems. Biomimicry is a discipline that applies the principles, systems, processes, and elements of nature and translates them to business life and the same practices apply for (mostly technological) innovations. These solutions tend to be more sustainable. In other words, biomimicry takes solutions from nature and applies them to architecture, machine design, biochemistry, hydraulic and mechanical engineering, automotive and design.[144] Velcro, for example, is inspired by the burdock plant. Velcro is an invention of the Swiss Georges de Mestral. He was surprised how well the burduck stuck to the coat of his dog. Under a microscope, he discovered the small hooks and the extremities of the plant which gave him the idea for inventing velcro. In its professional practice, HR can also use the ecosystem to come up with sustainable solutions for the increasingly complex work group problems.

Business ecosystem: Moving beyond traditional silos

It was James F. Moore who introduced the concept of a business ecosystem in an article that appeared in 1993 in the *Harvard Business Review*: "Predators and Prey: A New Ecology of Competition."[145] He later expanded on it in his 1996 book, *The Death Of Competition—Leadership And Strategy In The Age Of Business Ecosystems.*[146] Successful companies adapt rapidly and effectively, but—according to Moore—they can't evolve in a vacuum. Just like an ecosystem in nature can completely disappear due to extreme climate circumstances, so can organizations become irrelevant as the external context changes dramatically.

> **Strategically, organizations (and also HR) must have alignment and fit in their processes and procedures.**

The different HR and other business activities must be aligned and fit. Inside the organization the different management activities must be reconciled (alignment) and outside of the organization they must be adapted to the ever changing context (fit). To survive, organizations must—just like in nature—co-evolve in networks and ecosystems that go beyond their firm, industry or sector. Such innovative organizations use boundary spanning, which means they open their borders and bridge them.

There are five kinds of boundaries: vertical boundaries (hierarchies), horizontal boundaries (functions and expertise), stakeholder boundaries (external actors), demographic boundaries (gender, ethnicity, nationality) and geographic boundaries. To find solutions for complex problems, organizations must build relations and share knowledge across these boundaries.[147]

Organizations who move beyond the classic boundaries of their own firm, industry, and disciplinary silos unite in ecosystems where they develop innovative solutions for themselves and their stakeholders.

From egosystem to ecosystem

Ecosystems can play a central role in generating a competitive advantage. They generate value for all stakeholders who are part of the system and the final-end customer benefits. In contrast to subcontractor partnerships or static contractual partnerships, an ecosystem is changeable, changing, and therefore organic. The purpose of an ecosystem is that all members grow and win.

The idea of cooperation, partnerships, networks, and ecosystems is definitely not new, but its importance is growing. This is what we mean when we speak of the mindset of a *#ZigZagHR*-Ecosystem.

Get out of the building. The new value is not inside, it's at the edges of the network

Typical of an ecosystem mindset is the conviction that no organization stands by itself, but is part of a broader ecosystem and that solutions are usually found on the boundaries of and the cooperation with other organizations outside of one's own company.

> # Organizations with an ecosystem mindset put emphasis on building and maintaining long-term relations with actors outside of their company in the domains in which they are active. This means they continuously interact with others and this freedom is not limited to the CEO or the executive team, but is applicable to everyone in the organization. Everyone can look for things outside and bring them inside.

Do you sometimes have a feeling that you are stuck, that you can't breathe, that you are not able to innovate within your organization? A first important step is to open the door and bring the outside in. If you embrace this mindset, you will personally grow professionally and, as you grow, the organization will grow as well.

In *How an Ecosystem Mindset Can Help People and Organizations Succeed*, which appeared in a *Harvard Business Review* blog, John Geraci describes how you as an individual or a company can evolve from a closed organism mindset to an open ecosystem mindset.[148] And, by the way, you don't need to have a huge budget at your disposal to start using the principles underlying the ecosystem mindset. What you need is to:

- **REACH OUT**—connect with as many stakeholders as possible by organizing "let's go outside" events and hosting them.
- **SET UP CHANNELS**—always develop activities with the intention to cooperate even if it does not immediately lead to concrete business deals.
- **PARTNER**—with people that have totally different backgrounds.

And that is exactly what we have in mind for *#ZigZagHR*!

The idea of an ecoystem

is definitely not new,

but its importance is growing.

#ZigZagHR-ecosystem

We have the ambition to set up an (international) *#ZigZagHR*-Ecosystem: a dynamic, heterogeneous, and diverse community of progressive HR professionals AND non-HR professionals in different countries. Such a community evolves as the context evolves and as the new context brings challenges, it evolves and responds as well. The stakeholders of the *#ZigZagHR*-Ecosystem are, by design and preference, extremely diverse with regard to background, sector, activity, and life stage. It is our ambition to share with each other ideas, failures, and services within this *#ZigZagHR*-Ecosystem and to develop products and solutions that make each stakeholder better and produces a synergy that no stakeholder would be able to realize working alone.

A lot is expected from HR today as if HR professionals are super humans. In the meantime, many HR practitioners are still working in limiting and even sometimes toxic workplace environments.[149] By a toxic workplace environment, we mean a work environment with internal struggles. Toxic workplaces are usually the result of toxic employers, managers, and/or employees who are motivated in the first place by personal gain (power, money, fame, or special status), who use unethical and sometimes illegal methods to manipulate people and who are mainly interested in self aggrandizement. A poisonous workplace is destructive for employees and usually is experienced as a violation of the psychological contract with their employer. In the United States, the problem of harassment and bullying is getting more and more attention in the media. In the meantime, everyone pushes and pulls HR, but HR sits in the middle of it all and cannot always impact what's going on.

Climbing a mountain is done step by step. We love to make an analogy to the famous (and infamous) three-week long bicycle race, the *Tour de France*. The Tour has 21 stages and three weeks of treacherous cycling. No cyclist is capable of riding all these kilometers (or miles) in one big race!

> **We like to send the message to HR that climbing a mountain is done step by step.**

This book is the start of an international *#ZigZagHR*-Ecosystem, rather than a one-way street where the writer writes and the reader reads, where the best and leading HR practices don't necessarily originate in the Anglo-Saxon countries (mainly the U.S. and the U.K.) but blow over from all over the world.

This book is also a work in progress. Each time we finished a chapter, it already seem antiquated and we hear and read about new best and next practices, and each solution triggers another question. Each HR management book should in its next edition add an annex with forward-looking insights gained through the feedback the authors receive from the interactions with their readers—both HR professionals and non-HR professionals.

We will get to work too and apply the principles of an ecosystem mindset and bring people together in *#ZigZagHR*-Bootcamps, *#ZigZagHR*-Learning safaris, *#ZigZagHR*-Workshops and *#ZigZagHR*-Inspiration sessions, virtually as well as face-to-face.

Back to innovation and Peter Hinssen

Peter Hinssen's "day after tomorrow" model is genial and simple: to survive anno 2018, it is necessary to simultaneously be committed to exploration (the search for innovation) and exploitation (optimizing operational business management). Organizations must be both efficient enough to survive (today) and pay attention to innovation, so that in the future they continue to exist (the day after tomorrow).[150] In other words, organizations must strive to be ambidextrous if they want to be successful.

Ambi-what? The term ambidextrous is etymologically derived from the Lain word *ambos*, which means "both" and *dexter* meaning "right". Ambidextrous means something like having two right hands or, applied to organizations, being good at two widely divergent activities: optimizing versus innovating, short term versus long term, efficiency versus creativity and innovation. Ambidexterity requires one to simultaneously execute and manage two very different activities that demand different structures, processes and cultures, while managing the tension between the contradictions and finding the right balance. Concretely, this means one must not only pay time and attention to the day-to-day operational activities, but also invest sufficient time and resources in radical innovation. For most companies and (HR) people, this is a difficult balance to strike.

Beyond ambidexterity

Of course, most organizations know that intuitively. But only few succeed at it. The Peter Hinssen model is all but simple to put into practice because the idea of ambidexterity does not jive well with what we have learned about managing organizations; namely that as a company, one must get a competitive advantage. Either we compete on cost (operational excellence & exploitation), on customization (customer intimacy, value, innovation and exploration), or technology and production quality (product leadership). It also has to do with the fact that exploration and exploitation compete for resources with one another in terms of time, money, and people. An ambidextrous organization needs managers who master and optimize processes and simultaneously give direction to adopt uncertain innovative processes. An ambidextrous organization demands a different structure and culture and a total management approach that goes beyond the people on the payroll. An ambidextrous organization demands the letting go of a paternalistic HR approach vis-à-vis co-workers with rigid job descriptions. An ambidextrous organization requires that HR let go of certain processes, policies, procedures and work rules that were originally intended and designed to help people—because they curtail people. An ambidextrous organizations demands a new set of HR competencies on top of the existing HR BoK.

▊ **An ambidextrous organization needs #ZigZagHR...**

#How_do_we_do_that?

Create the future, forget the past, and manage the present

Managing the day-to-day operation of the business demands a totally different skill set, another leadership style, other metrics, and another mindset than managing non-linear radical innovation. Managing operational vs. innovation are two completely different challenges.

▊ **And the greatest stretch is the fact that people in organizations must do both at the same time.**

But, how do you that? How do we reinvent the existing business model while at the same time optimize the existing business?

It's not just about reinventing your business model and being committed to optimizing your current business model at the same time. It's really about—and probably especially about—letting go of deeply held convictions and creating processes that ensure the company and HR don't stay stuck and resist any form of radical innovation.
One of the HR managers of a Belgian firm recently described this challenge as follows: the company was at the top of its game for years, but recently is experiencing difficulties. She describes that it feels like being in airplane, high up in the sky at cruising speed. The last couple of years, there were no investment made in the plane, and temporary band-aid solutions (incremental innovation) were chosen because they seemed sufficient at the time. Now, one of the airplane doors seems like it is held together with duct tape. And still, there is no investment! Why not? Because theoretically, it is almost impossible for the airplane door to open in mid air. When

cruising at high altitude, the difference in pressure between the outside and the inside ensures, in principle, the door cannot open. In other words, there is no burning platform, no reason to change.

Vijaj Govindarajan and Chris Trimble conducted research for over 35 years on how, figuratively, not to remain seated in the airplane. They show organizations who don't (can't or wont) succeed in reinventing themselves and invest in the future in a timely manner, they continue to remain stuck in the operational part of the business and constantly have to extinguish fires.

> # Obviously, managing the current business and continuously improving is crucial: Your current business is the performance engine. It funds both day-to-day operations and generates profits for the future. Unfortunately, you cannot spend all your time, money, energy, and resources in that. Not all the people in your organization can exclusively focus on current operations.

Govindarajan and Trimble developed the "three box" model we mentioned before.[151] This model picks up the thread where Peter Hinssen left. It provides a framework for organizations, executives, and managers on how to spend available time, resources, means, and energy, divided over three boxes. It also explores opportunities for an innovative future while at the same time have a more performing answer to the challenges of today.

- **BOX 1**: Manage the present—improve the performance of your core business.
- **BOX 2**: Selectively forget the past—overcome your dominant logic (ways of doing things).
- **BOX 3**: Create the future—focus on truly innovative ideas that could fundamentally change your business.

In box 1, all your attention is focused on the short-term needs of your stakeholders. The focus here is on exploitation, optimization, and linear innovation. The mindset is on doing it faster, smarter and cheaper.

In box 2 (the past always fights back), time and space is freed up to support and create non-linear innovation. Here, barriers must be cut down.

In box 3, all attention is on experimentation. This is where the added value is created.

To get to the future, you must build it day by day

Govindarajan and Trimble's model is based on the belief that the future is not far away and it doesn't suddenly submerge us in a tsunami, but that the future is something one builds day after day. This means certain approaches and practices that once were successful must be set aside and make room for new practices.

#ZigZagHR is not a plea for *tabula rasa*—to throw the baby away with the bathwater—but a call to let go of things that no longer have added value for HR internal and external customers and the organization's stakeholders. Just as box 2 obstructs innovation, it also prevents HR from inventing a new role.

When do you start?

That's easy. When it's not necessary. Unfortunately many people only get into action when there is a burning platform; when there is an urgent need of an extinguisher; when it is already too late; when there is an urgency; when there is a crisis or life-or-death moment. Ultimately, building the future must be done constantly.

The sweet spot of optionality

"The big lesson I learned is that whatever the business – no matter how great it is, it is not always going to be a great business and you need to start thinking about that and planning for changes, when things are going well." (Mark Leslie)

One of the most influential blogs Mark Leslie, a docent in Entrepreneurship & Corporate Innovation at the Stanford Graduate School of Business, wrote, *The Arc of Company Life, and How to Prolong It*. Reviewing the four phases that each company typically goes through (start-up > growth > peak > decline), she argues that companies cannot wait to innovate until they are in the decline phase—even when they are at their peak, it is already too late. The sweet spot of optionality, as Leslie calls it – is the moment your company is doing really well and in full growth mode. She claims that if you can do that systematically, your organization has found the fountain of eternal corporate youth.[152]

> **Organizations are almost exclusively working in box 1: managing the present.**

This is logical because this is where organizations are in their comfort zone (and usually that is the cash cow). Here, they do what they have always done and try to optimize it. There are processes in place and they can rely on familiar structures. Everything is relatively controllable. It is important the employees who deal with box 1 challenges can focus on the processes and are not preoccupied with innovation or a complete rethink of the business model. One cannot expect the radical innovations to come from them. But from them, one can expect that they continuously improve and optimize the processes, because the revenue they generate is necessary to fund radical innovation.

Another reason why organizations are almost exclusively devoting their time and energy in box 1 and don't invest in the future is because they are not yet bothered by it today. When you neglect the future today, you don't see the damage today. One of the solutions is planned opportunism or a culture of active innovation where you are engaged in developing and attracting a fundamentally different set of skills and expertise. It is impossible to predict the future, but it is possible to prepare oneself for different (un)likely scenarios by attracting people who are working on that exclusively.

This brings us to box 3: creating the future.

> **Nothing is familiar, controllable, or predictable in box 3! Here organizations must experiment, while mistakes can (and must!) be made without blaming someone.**

The more successful organizations are in what they do, the harder it is to focus on box 3. Engaging in box 3 thinking requires letting go of certain beliefs, practices, and processes. As an HR manager in an IT company described: it requires to always look outside through the window so that you see and know what is changing; you must allow people to venture outside and bring the outside back in. Investing daily in box 3 prepares you for future scenarios that the context brings.

> **In box 2, the focus lies on "selectively" forgetting the past. Again, this does not mean tabula rasa because many processes that are in the way of radical innovation in box 3 still have utility in box 1.**

You're always

managing the present,

destroying the past,

and building the future.

However, this does mean that a distinction must be made between roots and chains, between timely and timeless values. If one completely destroys the roots of a tree, the tree will die. For HR and the business, it ultimately comes to identifying which assumptions, processes, and competencies obstruct the radical reinvention of your business model– and to eliminate them in box 2. Most organizations are not aware that some deep-rooted assumptions smother any form of radical innovation. The more attention that gets paid to this box, the greater the probability your business model can be radically reinvented.

The three-box model requires that managers and leaders are willing and capable of simultaneously thinking and working in these three time frames. This model requires that there are opportunities and formal processes to do so. In addition, the model is cyclical. The business models, the products and services that are created in box 3, will one day be in box 1. Depending on the context, the focus will have to be, sometimes more on box 1 or on box 3. If you succeed, you are building the future day by day.

#ZigZagHR and "the three boxes"

HR can also apply the three-box model:

- **BOX 1** means for HR to manage all HR activities that bring added value and are required for compliance. They optimize these activities and make them more efficient and effective, usually by augmenting it with IT tools (computers, robots, and algorithms).
- **BOX 2** means that HR is letting go of HR activities that no longer add value.
- **BOX 3** means that HR creates innovative HR activities to serve the stakeholders and future proof itself.

HR must be agile enough to strategically *#ZigZag* between holding on, letting go and innovating. Put on a pair of *#ZigZagHR* glasses and audit all your activities (processes, policies, and procedures) and the touchpoints that people have with your HR department. Even better, make it a disruptive audit! This will provide you with insights, challenges, and opportunities for your future HR. This requires that HR looks outside and searches which evolutions and technologies will have an impact on the organization and looks for any indication for potential innovation. HR must engage in a dialog with all its stakeholders: (potential) workers, clients, competitors, suppliers, unions, and other (HR) people through professional organizations and networks. Therefore, it is so important that you participate in a *#ZigZagHR*-Ecosystem.

In box 3, HR is required to experiment with non-linear innovation. For this, HR relies best on weak signals,[153] so the new competencies we described in the *#ZigZagHR*-Stack are required. Weak signals, are observations that warn us of possible future events. Finding relevant weak signals is one of the most challenging tasks in futurology and in organizations because the analysis often leads to the identification of the next big thing or opportunities that others have not yet detected. It is not because you pick up on such ambiguous signals that you know what to do with it. Most people negate that kind of information because it does not (yet) conform with their reality or needs. HR specialists and generalists may not pick up these signals, but mavericks and learnatics will. They often see the bigger picture and because of their insatiable desire to learn, they not only see signals, but they also connect the dots. Subsequently, this allows them to bring the outside in to generate solutions. They function perfectly well under great uncertainty, take risks, and make decisions based on incomplete information. They bring new competencies in house so that HR can reinvent itself.

In box 2, HR must let go of the processes and practices that no longer add value and become aware of beliefs (often unconscious) that stand in the way of innovation. The story of the caged monkey and the banana is a telling metaphor. A banana is suspended over stairs in a monkey cage. Quickly, one of the monkeys climbs the stairs, but as soon as the monkey tries to climb all the other monkeys are sprayed with water. Later, another monkey tries with the same results—all the monkeys are sprayed with water! A bit later, when another monkey wants to climb the stairs, the other monkeys hold him back. Now we replace one monkey in the cage with a new monkey. The new monkey soon goes up the stairs to get the banana, but the others immediately hold him back because they don't all want to be hosed again. Then, we replace another monkey with a new one in the cage. As soon as she climbs the stairs, she is attacked by the other monkeys—even though the new monkey who has no idea why she is being held back. And so its continues until all the old original monkeys have been replaced with new monkeys. The result: no monkeys ever dares climbing the stairs![154]

This often happens in organizations and in HR teams. We proverbially need monkeys who climb the stairs and dare ask critical questions when they are not allowed to. Years ago, Jef Staes described the resistance to innovation—with a dose of humor—by using the metaphor of the red monkeys and the organization as their jungle. His 2007 trilogy, *My Organization is a Jungle, I was the Lamb and my Manager was the Hero*, is still valid today.[155]

It should be obvious by now that one of the most important competencies HR needs to have when operating in the three boxes is change management. Using the distinction between causal and effectual thinking, ideas that originated at the turn of 21st century in the work of Saras D. Sarvasty,[156] we apply these different ways of thinking to two distinctive change management approaches that require different skillsets. Causal thinkers approach change management as a waterfall project, while effectual thinkers use a more agile approach. Causal change management thinking is more suited to box 1 (keep), while an effectual change management approach works better in box 3 (start).

Causal change management usually starts by what "is" and use a step-wise improvement methodology (whether TQM, Lean Six Sigma, PROSCI) to manage and implement a change initiative that "should" be. In doing so, they focus heavily on working through and with those who resist the change and try to avoid the most common mistakes identified by change management expert John Kotter.[157] This is the standard change management discipline taught in most business schools. It is very suitable to bring continuous improvement changes in box 1.

Effectual change management usually doesn't start from a clearly-defined goal. Instead, the change emerges more organically out of an ideation process and they adjust the change initiative in a more agile way as they progress. We refer here to the discussion we had about rapid prototyping when talking about agile HR. This type of change management initiative is more suited for box 3 for reengineering and entrepreneurial activities.

IN SUMMARY

This is a golden era for HR and an opportunity to reinvent people management by strategically *#ZigZagging* from traditional to more progressive HR practices. HR can become the catalyst for change by analyzing what they are currently doing, what they probably should no longer be doing, and what innovative activities they can start doing. The three-box model of Govindarajan and Trimble offers a simple and achievable roadmap for HR to apply innovation to themselves. By joining in a *#ZigZagHR*-Ecosystem, HR can get together with professionals from other management disciplines to develop solutions that benefit all stakeholders and that no single stakeholder could realize as well working on their own. *#ZigZagHR* is a framework that each organization can draw out using a simple rule of three that is both connected with and has an impact on the culture and the structure of the organization: (1) Continue to hold onto those HR activities that still add value and are required for compliance; (2) Stop and let go of HR activities that no longer add value or can be done quicker and better perhaps by algorithms; (3) Start and experiment with new and innovative HR practices.

Epilogue

STARTING A MOVEMENT WITH
THE *#ZIGZAGHR*-MANIFESTO

> **Joining the *#ZigZagHR*-Ecosystem is not without obligation. If you engage, you sign our *#ZigZagHR*-Manifesto!**

Why this manifesto? We are 100% convinced (and perhaps more) that HR can (and must) make the difference in organizations. But ideas are only that! If we want to start a movement and transform these ideas into concrete action, we must have believers and followers.

You probably have heard of Derek Sivers[158] and his brilliant TED Talk about "Leadership Lessons from the Dancing Guy." The key takeaway of this (very short)) TED Talk is: Leadership is overglorified. It's about the (first) follower(s). Therefore, we call on you to join our *#ZigZagHR*-Ecosystem.

Did you nod your head while reading this book?
Are you enthusiastic to get to work on some of those ideas?

> **Then, join our *#ZigZagHR*-Ecosystem!**

Have the courage to follow us and show others how to follow. Have the grinta to stand up and join in. Together, we can re-shape the future of HR.

With this *#ZigZagHR*-Manifesto, we put into words why we plead for *#ZigZagHR* and for a *#ZigZagHR*-Ecosystem and why we believe in it.

#ZigZagHR-Manifesto

1. Adopt a growth mindset
2. Get out & move
3. Connect
4. Learn
5. Break the silos
6. Experiment
7. Define, measure, and implement
8. Share lessons learned
9. Believe in serendipity
10. Find the HR sweet spot

Have the courage to follow us and show others how to follow. Have the *grinta* to stand up and join in. Together, we can re-shape the future of HR.

#*ZIGZAGHR*-MANIFESTO #1: ADOPT A GROWTH MINDSET

▌ **It's a great time to be in HR.**

If you join the *#ZigZagHR*-Ecosystem, you have to be convinced that HR is on the move; this is a new era and the time is now to reinvent HR. No Calimero stories, no stuck-in-the-middle sagas, but a proud and passionate attitude, eager to lead with a rebellious edge. We expect that you embrace a growth mindset and look at HR with a Pipi Longstocking bravado, because the way you look at HR determines how you develop yourself and the future of the profession.

#*ZIGZAGHR*-MANIFESTO #2: GET OUT & MOVE

If you want to join the *#ZigZagHR*-Ecosystem, it is important that you get out of your HR silo, literally as well as figuratively.

▌ **Get out!**
Get out of your own way.
Get out of your comfort zone.
Get out of HR and the office.

If we really want to reinvent HR and adopt the *#ZigZagHR* ideas in our organizations, we must search for ways to keep our promises to our stakeholders today and we must, at the same time, understand and supplement their future expectations. So, when we say get out, we mean we have to let go of our own closed mindset, break away from our familiar comfort zone (add a little *grinta* and a touch of *chutzpah*), but also liberate ourselves from structures, practices, and activities that work against it even if unintended. This is the only way HR can move and have an impact on the whole organization. This is the way HR can really make a difference and future proof itself.

#*ZIGZAGHR*-MANIFESTO #3: CONNECT

If you want to join the *#ZigZagHR*-Ecosystem, we expect that you have a connecting attitude with other HR (and non-HR) folks, wherever in the world, face-to-face and virtually. It is by connecting with like-minded and (especially) non-like minded people that you learn the most and gain new insights.

▌ **"Du choc des idées jaillit la lumière."**

Indeed, from the shock of ideas springs the light, or as the lyrics of one of Leonard Cohen's songs implies, "there is a crackin everything, that's how the light gets in." That is exactly what happened as a result of the collaboration of the authors of *#ZigZagHR*—and that is the added value of the *#ZigZagHR*-Ecosystem.

#ZIGZAGHR-MANIFESTO #4: LEARN

By connecting, we are constantly learning and getting new insights in other points of view, experiences, and disciplines. Joining the *#ZigZagHR*-ecosystem means that you sign onto life-long learning as a starting point to further develop as an HR professional. Use the following question when learning something new as they are the basis of developing life-long learning skills:

> **What is my major takeaway from this?**
> **What do I already know about this subject?**
> **What follow-up questions do I have about this?**
> **How can I apply this to HR in real life?**

For those who are not schooled in HR, this means gaining proficiency in the HR BoK through, for example, studying for an official HR certification or getting education and training to work in HR. For HR professionals, this means acquiring knowledge beyond HR; in other words outside of the traditional HR silo.

#ZIGZAGHR-MANIFESTO #5: BREAK THE SILOS

In a *#ZigZagHR*-Ecosystem, we accept that the best HR may no longer come from HR. We break industrial, sectorial, and functional silos; are open for knowledge and skills outside our management domain; and apply and integrate them into our HR practice. When you join the *#ZigZagHR*-Ecosystem, you look and go beyond the conventional. You look further, a bit deeper, and take another step. For us, it means you realize the importance of building bridges between HR and other management disciplines. Beyond means you leave the well-worn paths and choose resolutely for uncertainty and adventure. Beyond means for us that you learn to look over the wall.

#ZIGZAGHR-MANIFESTO #6: DEFINE, MEASURE, AND IMPLEMENT NEW IDEAS

By entering the *#ZigZagHR*-Ecosystem you handle all your HR activities with a "define, measure, and implement" rule of thumb:

- **DEFINE**: Define what the management concept that you use means in your organization (conceptualizations).
- **MEASURE**: Determine how you will measure the concept (operationalization).
- **IMPLEMENT**: Last but not least, you must be able to implement and execute the HR activity (support).

In other words, to determine whether a certain HR activity is successful, we must first conceptualize it within our own context (company culture, industry, sector, country location, etc.). Then, we need metrics to measure success. Finally, we need the necessary structures and resources to support and scale the activity.

#ZIGZAGHR-MANIFESTO #7: EXPERIMENT

By joining the #ZigZagHR-Ecosystem, you are open for experimentation because ideas only get you so far, right? Experimentation goes a bit further than innovation! Thomas Edison said, "Innovation is 1% inspiration and 99% perspiration." And he was right. Bringing creative and diverse people together in your company and organizing brainstorm sessions will, for sure, increase the number of innovative ideas. However, this is no guarantee for effective execution. That requires experimentation to see whether the new idea works and responds to the wants and needs of the different personas in organizations and the agility to discontinue it if it doesn't work. A/B-testing is a basic form of experimentation and can give us the needed evidence to support HR decisions.

> **Coming up with a wild idea is very sexy, but the execution of that wild idea is more difficult and can, according to us, not be done solo or in a vacuum. Therefore, we want to bundle our forces across the HR boundaries and organize ourselves into a #ZigZagHR-Ecosystem for added support.**

#ZIGZAGHR-MANIFESTO #8: SHARE LESSONS LEARNED

A #ZigZagHR-Ecosystem is a network of diverse people who do not only share their ideas but also best practices and lessons learned. The time of blindly taking over best practices from other companies in a copy-past format—no matter how good these practices might be—is over. Networking does not solely mean, "what I can get from other?" But, more so, "what can I offer others?' Be inquisitive, listen to your environment and handle intellectual flexibility.

> **Joining our #ZigZagHR-Ecosystem means that your share your knowledge and experiences, explicit as well as tacit knowledge, with a network of HR and non-HR colleagues in and outside the walls of your company.**

#*ZIGZAGHR*-MANIFESTO #9: BELIEVE IN SERENDIPITY

> **Serendipity: Finding something good or beautiful without looking for it.**

Serendipity is at the origin of many discoveries that were done by chance. Leo Baekelandt's name is connected with the discovery of bakelite (the precursor of plastic) in 1909. Alexander Fleming, by coincidence discovered penicillin in 1928 and Percy Spencer invented the microwave oven in 1945. Hedy Lamarr was the co-inventor of 1940 wireless technology that later became the foundation of mobile phone technology. Grace Hopper invented the first computer code that led to the development of coding language. More recently in 1968, Spencer Silver came up with post-it notes.

Serendipity is of great value in a business context as the capacity for knowledge creation often passes through tacit knowledge—and sometimes very subjective insights, intuitions, and promptings of individual workers—rather than by processing existing information. When employee insights are shared with the team they are made available to the entire enterprise. If you want to join the *#ZigZagHR*-Ecosystem, embrace your serendipity.

#*ZIGZAGHR*-MANIFESTO #10: FIND THE SWEET SPOT

Finally, joining the *#ZigZagHR*-Ecosystem means that you handle your HR activities with strong ethical values, whatever the situation dictates. Our most difficult HR decisions are made when the requirements of the stakeholders are in conflict with one another. We always must aim for the sweet spot, where what is good for the worker is also good for the customer and the organization. Therefore, we can never forget that the H in HR stands for human!

Here's to the rebels

"Here's to the crazy ones, the misfits, the rebels, the troublemakers, the round pegs in the square holes, the ones who see things differently – they're not always fond of rules! You can quote them, disagree with them, glorify or vilify them, but the only thing you can't do, is ignore them because they change things. They push the human race forward, and while some may see them as the crazy ones, we see genius, because the ones who are crazy enough to think that they can change the world, are the ones who do it."

You'll be the judge if this quote really belonged to Steve Jobs or was written by the marketing team for Apple's "Think Different" campaign. But it perfectly fits the description of HR rebel or *#ZigZagHR* professionals.

Join the movement and join our *#ZigZagHR-Ecosystem*!

Lisbeth & Lesley

Acknowledgements

We are grateful for the professional friendship and support of the following people: Luc De Decker (HR Square, Belgium), Scott Baker (Vice President People for Command Alkon, Birmingham, Alabama, USA), and Carol Olsby (Managing Director, Carol Olsby & Associates, Chair, Global HR Consortium/IT Roundtable, Redmond, Washington, USA).

Lisbeth dedicates this book to An Verbeke, her Belgian high school teacher and role model who already in 1968 showed what it really means to be a *straffe madam*.

Lesley dedicates this book to all HR rebels who have inspired her to write this book and to her husband Sven Hubin, because it was undoubtedly also exhausting for him.

#ZigZagHR-Toolkit

RETHINK, RETOOL, REBOOT

Lisbeth Claus has designed a number of tools to introduce the #ZigZagHR-Stack to HR practitioners and students. These tools—originally developed for her global HR courses in the Willamette MBA—can be used and adapted for learning and development events with your HR team.

#ZigZagHR-Toolkit to introduce design thinking in HR.
- Employee experience mapping
- Touchpoint management
- Rapid prototyping

ZigZagHR-Toolkit to introduce agile lite to your HR team.
- User stories
- Sprint release planning
- Stand-up meetings

ZigZagHR-Toolkit to introduce behavioral economics to HR.
- Unconscious bias
- Nudging
- Search advocate

ZigZagHR-Toolkit to apply analytics to HR.
- Evidence-based HR
- Data mining
- Sentiment analysis
- A/B testing

ZigZagHR-Toolkit to apply the principles of global standardization vs. local responsiveness to HR.

ZigZagHR-Toolkit to use the three boxes in HR.

In line with the *#ZigZagHR*-Ecosystem, Lisbeth gladly makes these tools available to interested HR practitioners, HR teams, trainers and academic instructors. Please contact her on LinkedIn.

Biography of the Authors

LISBETH CLAUS
Ph.D., SPHR, GPHR, SHRM-SCP

Dr. Lisbeth Claus (o1951, Oostende, Belgium) published more than 100 articles about international HR in academic and professional journals. She specializes in the implications for global organizations when their employees cross borders. She was co-author (with Dennis Briscoe and Randall Schuler) of the 3rd edition of *International Human Resource Management* (Routledge, 2008) and Editor-in-Chief of the four-volume *Global HR Practitioner Handbook* (Global Immersion Press, 2013, 2014, 2015, 2019).

Considered the premier global expert on employer duty of care, she traveled to four continents to inform employers of their obligation to protect their business travelers, international assignees, and dependents. She is the author of the 2009 International SOS *Duty of Care White Paper* viewed today as a major impetus for putting duty of care on the map for global organizations. She authored the 2012 *Duty of Care and Travel Risk Management Global Benchmarking Study*, the first empirical study on duty of care for which she earned the EMMA award for research of the year.

Other areas of research interest include developments in performance management, HR analytics, resilient career development, and the development of a culture of health and well being in international organizations

At its inaugural annual global HR conference in March 2016, the IT HR Roundtable/ Global HR Consortium announced the creation of the annual *Lisbeth Claus Trail Blazer Award* in honor of her life-long dedication to the development of the global HR profession around the world.

A native of Belgium, she is fluent in Flemish, French, and English and has a working knowledge of German.

Foremost an educator, she has inspired thousands of learners—graduate students and practitioners—to better navigate the global scope of management.

Contact: lclaus@willamette.edu

LESLEY ARENS

Lesley Arens (o1974, Gent, Belgium) does not have a classic educational trajectory but combined learning with work during her career. She breathes life-long learning. She interrupted her university studies to work in the restaurant business of her parents until at age 26, as a single mother, she returned to school with 18-year olds. At the same time, she taught weekend classes in adult education programs as part of teacher training. Although this was the most difficult period of her life, it was also the most rewarding.

As a child of independent small business owners, she started her formal career as a docent in adult education where she quickly moved on to become one of the executive members of the largest center for adult education (CVO) in Flanders. She was responsible for the implementation of training and development for the province of East Flanders and introduced the importance of customer orientation and customization in adult education.

Seven years later, as Managing Director of a consortium of adult education, she focused on strategic policy regarding adult education and life-long learning. She initiated and coordinated the cooperation among the centers of adult education, public education providers (such as VDAB and Syntra), sectors, companies, and other intermediary organizations. This made her discover the early forms of dual learning. She developed marketing and communication plans to promote life-long learning and increase the participation in adult education focusing on diversity and equal opportunities.

In 2014, she shifted her focus on learning and development in business joining the VOV, an organization focused on learning and development (L&D) of HR professionals. Under her leadership it became the model for everyone professionally involved in organizational development (OD), L&D, change, HR, and talent development with over 900 members. She organized monthly pitstops around current themes in L&D, OD and HRD, master classes with international experts and a bi-annual trade fairs for HR and L&D professionals in the Benelux.

In 2016, she started her own company "Connect and Learn" organizing exclusive network events on leadership, life-long learning, and HR and delivered inspirational keynotes on these topics. She was also a freelance business partner of HRbuilders where she connected employers with temporary HR staff and was responsible for content, social media, and client events.

Life-long learning, innovation, inspiring others, and networking are the leitmotiv in her #ZigZag-Career. She shares her vision in LinkedIn blogs and other forums.

Contact: lesley.arens@telenet.be

Notes

INTRODUCTION

Why we wrote #ZigZagHR

1.   Hinssen, P. (2017) *The Day After Tomorrow*: Hoe Overleven in Tijden van Radicale Innovatie. Leuven: LannooCampus/Van Duuren Management.

CHAPTER 1

Why #ZigZagHR?
A NEW WORLD, A NEW HR

2.   Gratton, L. (2011) *The Shift: The Future of Work is Already Here*. London: HarperCollins.
3.   Morgan, J. (2014) *The Future of Work: Attract New Talent, Build Better Leaders, and Create a Competitive Organization*. New York: John Wiley & Sons.
4.   Morgan, J. (2017) *The Employee Experience Advantage: How to Win the War for Talent by Giving Employees the Workspaces they Want, the Tools they Need, and a Culture they Can Celebrate*. New York: John Wiley & Sons.
5.   Bersin, J. (2016) *The Future Of work: It's Already Here – And Not as Scary as You Think*. https://www.forbes.com/sites/joshbersin/2016/09/21/the-future-of-work-its-already-here-and-not-as-scary-as-you-think/#701dec5f4bf5
6.   Claus. L. & Baker, S. (2018) 'The global HR stack: External and internal tools and methodologies impacting HR', pp. 35-63 in L. Claus (ed.), *Global HR Practitioner Handbook* (vol. 4), Silverton, OR: Global Immersion Press.
7.   Whiteman, W. E. (1998) *Training and Educating Army Officers for the 21st Century: Implications for the United States Military Academy*. Carlisles Barracks, PA: U.S. Army War College. http://www.dtic.mil/dtic/tr/fulltext/u2/a345812.pdf
8.   Johansen, B. (2017) *The New Leadership Literacies: Thriving in the Future of Extreme Disruption and Distributed Everything*. Oakland: Berrett-Koehler Publishers.
9.   Hinssen, P. (2017) *The Day After Tomorrow: Hoe Overleven in Tijden van Radicale Innovatie*. Leuven: LannooCampus/Van Duuren Management.
10. Morgan, J. (2017) *The Employee Experience Advantage: How to Win the War for Talent by Giving Employees the Workspaces they Want, the Tools they Need, and a Culture they Can Celebrate*. New York: John Wiley & Sons.
11. Gratton, L. & Scott, A, (2016) *The 100-Year Life: Living and Working in an Age of Longevity*. London: Bloomsbury Publishing.
12. Stewart, M. (2018) 'The birth of a new aristocracy: The gilded future of the top 10 percent – and the end of opportunity for everyone else', *The Atlantic*, June, pp. 48-63.

13. Browaeys, T. (2017) Statistieken burn-out: 'Eigenlijk willen we dit niet meer. *En toch gaan we door' Knack* 18/04/2017. http://www.knack.be/nieuws/gezondheid/statistieken-burn-out-eigenlijk-willen-we-dit-niet-meer-en-toch-gaan-we-door/article-opinion-841847.html

14. Kleinste personeelsverloop sinds 2007, Belgen blijven bij hun werkgever, *HR Square* 25/03/2016. http://www.hrsquare.be/nl/nieuws/kleinste-personeelsverloop-sinds-2007-belgen-blijven-bij-hun-werkgever.

15. Vandersijpe, F. & Bosmans, G. (2018), *Personeelsverloop in 2017: Vrijwillige verloop stagneert op dieptepunt ondanks record aantal vacatures.* Whitepaper Securex, April. file:///C:/Users/lesle/Downloads/18012.SECU.whitepaper.verloop_tofu2nl.pdf

16. Manning, A. (2003), *Monopsony in Motion: Imperfect Competition in Labor Markets*, Princeton: Princeton University Press.

17. Cappelli, P. (2008) 'Talent management for the twenty-first century', *Harvard Business Review*, March, 86: 3, pp. 74–81.

18. *Freelancing in America 2017 Report*. https://www.upwork.com/i/freelancing-in-america/2017/

19. Anseel, F., Ducheyne, D., Vander Sijpe, F. & Vossaert, L. (2018) *Personaliseren van Werk: Mythes & Feiten*. Leuven: Acco.

20. Boulton, S. & Houlihan, M. (eds.), (2007) *Searching for the Human in Human Resource Management: Theory, Practice and Workplace Contexts*. London: Palgrave.

21. Hinssen, P. (2017) *The Day After Tomorrow: Hoe Overleven in Tijden van Radicale Innovatie*. Leuven: LannooCampus/Van Duuren Management.

22. Graham, P. (2012) *How to Get Startup Ideas*. www.paulgraham.com/startupideas.html

CHAPTER 2

#ZigZagHR-Model
BECAUSE HR MUST (DARE-WANT-MAY-CAN) COLOR OUTSIDE OF THE LINES

23. Hammonds. K.H. (2005) 'Why we hate HR', *Fast Company*, August, pp. 40-47.

24. Cappelli, P. (2015) 'Why we love to hate HR… and what HR can do about it', *Harvard Business Review*, July-August, 93: 7/8, pp. 54-61.

25. Charan, R. (2014) 'It's time to split HR', *Harvard Business Review*, July-August, 92: 7/8, pp. 34-34.

26. Cohen, D. (2007) 'The very separate worlds of academic and practitioner publications in human resource management: Reasons for the divide and solutions for bridging the gap', *Academy of Management Journal*, 50: 5, pp. 1013-1019.

27. Govindarajan, V. & Trimble, C. (2011) 'The CEO's role in business model reinvention', *Harvard Business Review*. January-February, 89: 1/2, pp. 108-114.

28. Quinn, R.E. & Thakor, A. V. (2018) 'Creating a purpose-driven organization', *Harvard Business Review*, July-August, 96: 4, pp. 78-85.

29. Schein, E. H. (2010) *Organizational Culture and Leadership*. (4th edition) San Francisco: John Wiley & Sons.

30. Kim. W.C. & Mauborgne, R. (2005) *Blue Ocean Strategy: How to Create Uncontested Market Space and Make the Competition Irrelevant*. Boston: Harvard Business School Press.

31. Claus, L. (2014) 'Global talent management', pp. 116-131 in L. Claus (ed.), *Global HR Practitioner Handbook* (vol. 1), Silverton: Global Immersion Press.

32. Ulrich, D. & Brockbank, W. (2005) *The HR Value Proposition*. Boston: Harvard Business School Press.

33. Boulton, S. & Houlihan, M. (eds.), (2007) *Searching for the Human in Human Resource Management: Theory, Practice and Workplace Contexts*. London: Palgrave.

CHAPTER 3

#ZigZagHR-Workforce
THE FUTURE OF WORK: FLEXIBILITY AND A HYBRID WORKFORCE

34. Goldsmith, M. & Reiter, M. (2008) *What Got You Here, Won't Get You There: How Successful People Become Even More Successful*. Profile Books Ltd.

35. Sanders, I. & Sloly, D. (2012) *Mash-up! How to Use Your Multiple Skills to Give You an Edge, Make Money and Be Happier*. London: Kogan Page.

36. Werkbaar en Wendbaar Werk (2017) http://www.werk.belgie.be/defaultTab.aspx?id=45804

37. Gratton, L. & Scott, A, (2016) *The 100-Year Life: Living and Working in an Age of Longevity*. London: Bloomsbury Publishing.

38. McKinsey (2018) *How will automation effect economies around the world*. https://www.mckinsey.com/featured-insights/future-of-organizations-and-work/how-will-automation-affect-economies-around-the-world

39. Van Parijs, P & Vandenborght, Y. (2017) *Basic Income: a Radical Proposal for a Free Society and a Sane Economy*. Cambridge: Harvard University Press.

40. Willyerd, K. & Mistick, B. (2016) *Stretch: How to Future-Proof Yourself for Tomorrow's Workplace*. Hoboken: John Wiley & Sons.

41. Gustavo Razetti, (8 March 2018) *5 Steps to Reigniting Career Development for Today's Workforce*. https://www.linkedin.com/pulse/5-steps-reigniting-career-development-todays-gustavo/

42. Ries, E. (2011) *The Lean Startup: How Today's Entrepreneurs Use Continuous Innovation to Create Radically Successful Businesses*. New York: Crown Business Publishing Group.

43. Nixon, A & Claus, L. (2014). 'Global worklife balance and stress management', pp. 175-196 in L. Claus (ed.), *Global HR Practitioner Handbook* (vol. 1), Silverton: Global Immersion Press.

44. Willyerd, K. & Mistick, B. (2016) *Stretch: How to Future-Proof Yourself for Tomorrow's Workplace*. Hoboken: John Wiley & Sons.

45. Thomas, D. & Brown, J.S. (2011) *A New Culture of Learning: Cultivating the Imagination for a World of Constant Change*. Createspace.

46. Gallup, Inc. (2018). Gallup Daily: U.S. Employee Engagement, www.news.gallup.com/poll/180404/gallup-daily-employee-engagement.aspx.

47. Bailey, S. & Black, O. (2014) *Mind Gym: Achieve More by Thinking Differently*. New York: Harper Collins.

48. Mikkelsen, K. & Martin, R. (2016) *The Neo-Generalist: Where you go is who you are*. Lid Publishing.

49. HR Square Conference (2017) 'Duizend tinten medewerkers', Bad Neuenahr – Ahrweiler, Duitsland, 19-21 oktober.

50. *Werknemersgroeperingen*. http://www.werk.belgie.be/defaultTab.aspx?id=43404

51. *Co-sourcing*. SD Worx, https://www.sdworx.be/nl-be/sd-worx-consulting/oplossingen/co-sourcing; Pollentier, B. (2014) *Co-sourcing and pooling: Mobiliseren van talent*. sdworks 1 april. https://www.sdworx.be/nl-be/sd-worx-r-d/publicaties/artikels/co-sourcing-en-pooling-mobiliseren-van-talent; *Studie toont co-sourcing als oplossing voor langere loopbanen* (7 november 2017) sdworks, https://www.antwerpmanagementschool.be/pers/studie-toont-co-sourcing-als-oplossing-voor-langere-loopbanen/

52. *Freelancing in America 2017 Report* (2017), https://www.upwork.com/i/freelancing-in-america/2017/

53. *SERV-rapport* (2017), http://www.serv.be/stichting/publicatie/freelancers-vlaanderen)

54. Freelancers in Vlaanderen Stichting innovatie & arbeid (2017) http://www.serv.be/stichting/publicatie/freelancers-vlaanderen

55. Pollentier, B. (2014) *Co-sourcing and pooling: Mobiliseren van talent*. sdworks 1 april. https://www.sdworx.be/nl-be/sd-worx-r-d/publicaties/artikels/co-sourcing-en-pooling-mobiliseren-van-talent;

56. Mayika, J., Lundl, S., Bughin, J., Robinson, K., Mischke, J. & Mahajan, D. (2016) *Independent Work: Choice, Necessity, and the Gig Economy*. Report, McKinsey Global Institute, October. https://www.mckinsey.com/~/media/McKinsey/Global%20Themes/Employment%20and%20Growth/Independent%20work%20Choice%20necessity%20and%20the%20gig%20economy/Independent-Work-Choice-necessity-and-the-gig-economy-Executive-Summary.ashx).

57. Deleu, M. (2018) 'Op Zoek naar een Europees Beleid voor Freelancers', *Nextconomy*, 13 februari. https://www.nextconomy.be/2018/02/opzoek-naar-een-europees-beleid-voor-freelancers/

58. Nair, L. (2018) *Opening keynote speech*. Beyond: The Global HR Leadership Forum. https://www.beyondhrforum.com/speaker/leena-nair/

59. Ashford, K. (2016), 'How these millennials boosted their savings rates', *Forbes*, 28 April, https://www.forbes.com/sites/kateashford/2016/04/28/millennials-savings/#231558ef4a6c

60. Smeyers, L. (2018). *'Denk als een marketeer', HR Square*. Januari 2018, 176: pp. 14.

CHAPTER 4

#ZigZagHR-Stack
A NEW SKILLSET BEYOND HR

61. Claus. L. & Baker, S. (2018) 'The global HR stack: External and internal tools and methodologies impacting HR', pp. 35-63 in L. Claus (ed.), *Global HR Practitioner Handbook* (vol. 4), Silverton, OR: Global Immersion Press.

62. Archer, B. *Systematic Method for Designers* (1965). London: Council of Industrial Design.

63. Martin, R. (2009). *The Design of Business: Why Design Thinking is the Next Competitive Advantage*. Boston: Harvard Business Review Press.

64. Mazur, A.H., Zucker, J., Sivak, M., Coombes, R. & Van Durme, Y. (2017) *Reimagine and Craft the Employee Experience: Design Thinking in Action*. Deloitte Development LLC. https://www2.deloitte.com/content/dam/Deloitte/be/Documents/consulting/Deloitte%20%20Reimagine%20&%20Craft%20Employee%20Experience%20-%20Design%20Thinking%20in%20Action%20POV.pdf

65. Bersin, J., Solow, M. & Wakefield, N. (2016). *Design Thinking: Crafting the Employee Experience*. https://dupress.deloitte.com/dup-us-en/focus/human-capital-trends/2016/employee-experience-management-design-thinking.html.

66. Morgan, J. (2014) *The Future of Work: Attract New Talent, Build Better Leaders, and Create a Competitive Organization*. New York: John Wiley & Sons.

67. O'Connor, N. (2016) *How to Build an Experience Map*. https://medium.com@wnialloconnor/how-to-build-an-expereince-map-5e55b7ee43f32.January 25; Risdon, C. (2011) *The anatomy of an experience map*. http://adaptivepath.org/ideas/the-anatomy-of-an-experience-map/ November 30

68. Clapon, P. (2016) *Your Guide to Employee Experience Mapping*. http://www.gethppy.com/employee-engagement/guide-employee-experience-mapping; *Employee Journey Mapping* (2012) http://touchpointdashboard.com/2012/11/employee-journey mapping

69. Yohn, D.L. (2016). 'Design your employee experience as thoughtfully as you design your customer experience', *Harvard Business Review Human Resource Management blog*, December 8.

70. Mazur, A.H., Zucker, J., Sivak, M., Coombes, R. & Van Durme, Y. (2017) *Reimagine and Craft the Employee Experience: Design Thinking in Action*. Deloitte Development LLC. https://www2.deloitte.com/content/dam/Deloitte/be/Documents/consulting/Deloitte%20%20Reimagine%20&%20Craft%20Employee%20Experience%20-%20Design%20Thinking%20in%20Action%20POV.pdf

71. O'Connor, N. (2016) *How to Build an Experience Map*. https://medium.com@wnialloconnor/how-to-build-an-expereince-map-5e55b7ee43f32;

72. Risdon, C. (2011) *The Anatomy of an Experience Map*. http://adaptivepath.org/ideas/the-anatomy-of-an-experience-map/November 30

73. Kolko, J. (2015) 'Design thinking comes of age', *Harvard Business Review*, September, 93: 9, pp. 66-71.

74. Kelley, T. & Kelley, D. (2013) *Creative Confidence: Unleashing the Creative Potential within Us All*. New York: Crown Business.

75. Aghina, W., De Smet, A., Lackey G., Lurie, M. & Murarka, M. (2018) *The Five Trademarks of Agile Organizations*. MKinsey& Company. https://www.mckinsey.com/business-functions/organization/our-insights/the-five-trademarls-of- agile-organizations Rose, D. (2015) *Leading Agile Teams*. Newtown Square: Project Management Institute; Canty, C. (2015). *Agile for Project Managers*. Boca Raton: CBC Press.

76. Rose, D. (2015) *Leading Agile Teams*. Newtown Square: Project Management Institute; Canty, C. (2015) *Agile for Project Managers*. Boca Raton: CBC Press.

77. Rigby, D.K., Sutherland, J. & Takeuchi, H. (2016) 'Embracing Agile: How to master the process that's transforming management', *Harvard Business Review*, March, 94: 5, pp. 40-50.

78. Rose, D. (2015) *Leading Agile Teams*. Newtown Square: Project Management Institute; Canty, C. (2015). *Agile for Project Managers*. Boca Raton: CBC Press.

79. Cappelli, P. & Travis, A. (2018) 'HR goes Agile', *Harvard Business Review*, March-April, 96: 2, pp. 46-61.

80. Boskma, W., Buizer, M., van de Hoef, N, Peters, G. & Zelen, W. (2017) *Agile HR*. Nubiz.

81. *Principles Behind the Agile HR Manifesto*. http://www.agilehrmanifesto.org/principles-behind-the-hr-manifesto

82. Silim, A. (2017) *What is new economic thinking? Three strands of heterodox economics that are leading the way*. Evonomics, April 25. http://evonomics.com/new-economic-thinking/

83. Kahneman, D. (2011) *Thinking Fast and Slow*. London: Penguin Group.

84. Kahneman, D. & Tversky, A. (1983) 'Choices, values and frames', *The American Psychologist*, 39: 4, 341-350.

85. Tversky, A. & Kahneman, D. (1974) 'Judgment under uncertainty: Heuristics and biases', *Science, New Series*, 185: 4147, 1124-1131.

86. Thaler, R. &. Sunstein, C.S. (2008) *Nudge: Improving Decisions about Health, Wealth and Happiness*. New York: Penguin Books.

87. Ibid., p. 6.

88. Ibid., p. 8.

89. Ibid., p.11.

90. Ibid, p. 22.

91. Ibid, p. 24.

92. Claus, L., Baker, S. & Ely, J. (2015) 'Global HR analytics: Making grounded talent management decisions for the global organization', pp. 5-33 in Claus. L. (ed.), *Global HR Practitioner Handbook* (vol. 3), Silverton: Global Immersion Press.

93. Boudreau, J.W. & Ramstad, P.M. (2007). *Beyond HR: The New Science of Human Capital*. Boston: Harvard Business School Press.

94. Leonardi, P. & Contractor, N. (2018). 'Better People Analytics', *Harvard Business Review*, November-December, 96: 6, pp. 74-81.

95. Kohavi, R. & Thomke, S. (2017) 'The surprising power of online experiments', *Harvard Business Review*, September-October, 95: 5, pp.74-82.

96. Evans, P., Pucik, V. & Bjorkman, I. (2016) *The Global Challenge: Frameworks for International Human Resource Management* (3rd edition). Chicago: Business Press.

CHAPTER 5

#ZigZagHR-Career
HR MUST CHANGE INSIDE TO RESPOND TO DEMANDS FOR SOLUTIONS FROM OUTSIDE

97. Govindarajan, V. & Trimble, C. (2011) 'The CEO's role in business model reinvention', *Harvard Business Review*, January-February, 89: 1/2, pp. 108-114.

98. Ulrich, D. & Brockbank, W. (2005) *The HR Value Proposition*. Boston: Harvard Business School Press.

99. Herzberg, T. (2003). 'One more time: How do you motivate employees?', *Harvard Business Review*, January, 81: 1, pp. 87-96.

100. Van Dam, N. (2018) 'Learning in the digital age', *BizEd*, 1 March. https://bized.aacsb.edu/articles/2018/03/learning-in-the-digital-age

101. Boulton, S. & Houlihan, M. (eds.), (2007) *Searching for the Human in Human Resource Management: Theory, Practice and Workplace Contexts*. London: Palgrave.

102. Kühn, T. S. (1962) *The Structure of Scientific Revolutions*. Chicago: University of Chicago Press.

103. Morgan, J. (2014) *The Future of Work: Attract New Talent, Build Better Leaders, and Create a Competitive Organization*. New York: John Wiley & Sons.

104. Dweck, C. (2007) *Mindset: The New Psychology of Success*. New York: Ballantine Books.

105. Gulati, R. (2018) 'Structure that's not stifling', *Harvard Business Review*, May–June, 96: 3, pp.

106. Claus, L. (2007) *Scouting Talent at Google: Global Recruiting in Action* https://www.globalimmersionpress.com/collections/vignettes/products/scouting-talent-at-google-global-recruiting-in-action-1

107. Crosell, A. (2017) *5 Unique Human Resources Job Titles for 2017*. https://blog.cultureamp.com/5-unqie-humna-resources-job-titles-for-207

CHAPTER 6

#ZigZagHR-Operations
HOW HR ZIGZAGS BETWEEN TRADITIONAL AND PROGRESSIVE HR

108. Inkeles, A. (1964) *What is Sociology: an Introduction to the Discipline and Profession?* Englewood Cliffs: Prentice-Hall.

109. Wright, P., McMahan, G., Snell, S. & Gerhart, B. (1998) *Strategic HRM: Building Human Capital and Organizational Capabilities*. Ithaca: Cornell University, Technical Report.

110. Ulrich, D. & Brockbank, W. (2005) *The HR Value Proposition*. Boston: Harvard Business School Press.

111. Morgan, J. (2014) *The Future of Work: Attract New Talent, Build Better Leaders, and Create a Competitive Organization*. New York: John Wiley & Sons.

112. Boudreau, J.W. & Ramstad, P.M. (2007). *Beyond HR: The New Science of Human Capital*. Boston: Harvard Business School Press.

113. Ferrari, A. (2017) *These top HR Tech trends are revolutionizing the industry*. https://gocanvas.io/resources/these-top-hr-tech-trends-are-revolutionazing-the-industry. 10/16/2017; Milligan, S. (2017) 'HR Then and Now', *HR Magazine*, August 2015, pp. 38-41; Maier, S. (2017) *The top five HR Trends for 2017*. https/www.fastcompany.com/3066976/the-top-five-hr-rtrends-for-2017.

114. Buckingham, M. & Goodall, A. (2015) 'Reinventing performance management', *Harvard Business Review*, April, 93: 4, pp. 40-50; Chandler, M.T. (2016) *How Performance Management is Killing Performance—and What to do about It*. Oakland: Berrett-Koehler Publications.

115. Claus, L & Baker, S. (2016) 'The new global performance management paradigm—Reinventing performance reviews', pp.166-99 in Claus, L. (ed.), *Global HR Practitioner Handbook* (vol. 3), Silverton: Global Immersion Press.

116. *List of Minimum Annual Leave by Country* (2013) https://en.m.wikipedia.org/wiki/List_of_minimum_annual_leave_by_country; *Countries most Vacation Days* (2013) https://www.usatoday.com/story/money/business/2013/06/08/countries-most-vacation-days/2400193/

117. Castillo-Frick, I. (2017) 'The Evolution of Workflex', *HR Magazine*, December, pp. 30-31; *Latest Telecommuting Statistics* (2018) Global Workplace Analytics, http://globalworkplaceanalystics.com/telecommuting-statistics.

118. *10 Stats About Remote Work*. https://remote.co/10-stats-remote-work/

119. Spector, N. (2107) *Why are big companies calling their remote workers back to the office?* July 27. https://www.nbcnews.com/business/business-news/why-are-bg-compnaies-calling-their-remote-workers-back-oggvie-n787101

120. Van der Meulen, N. (2016) *The Distance Dilemma: The Effect of Flexible Working Practices on Performance in the Digital Workplace*. Doctoral Dissertation, Rotterdam: Erasmus University.

121. 'Firms should make more information about salaries public', *The Economist*, October 28, p. 71. https://www.economist.com/news/finance-and-economics/21730647-making-pay-more-transparent-firsms-should-make-more-infomration-about-salaries

122. Michaels, E., Handfield-Jones, H. & Axelrod, B. (2001) *The War for Talent*. Boston: Harvard Business School Press.

123. *Net Promoter Score*. http://netpromotersystem.com/about/employee-engagement.aspx

124. Morgan, J. (2017) *The Employee Experience Advantage: How to Win the War for Talent by Giving Employees the Workspaces they Want, the Tools they Need, and a Culture they Can Celebrate*. New York: John Wiley & Sons.

125. Gallup, Inc. (2018). *Gallup Daily: U.S. Employee Engagement*. Retrieved October 29, 2018 from www.news.gallup.com/poll/180404/gallup-daily-employee-engagement.aspx.

126. Green, D. & Stevens, L. (2018) *The Dos and Dont's of Continuous Listening*. https://www.linkedin.com/pulse/dos-donts-continuous-listening-david-green/

127. *SHRM Learning System* (2016) Alexandria: SHRM, p.131.

128. Crenshaw, K. (2016) *The Urgency of Intersectionality*. 7 December. https://www.youtube.com/watch?v=akOe5-UsQ2o

129. Simpson, J. (2009) *Everyone Belongs: A Toolkit for Applying Intersectionality*. CRIAW-ICREF. http://www.criaw-icref.ca/en/sites/criaw/files/Everyone_Belongs_e.pdf

130. Solomon, A. (2012) *Far from the Tree: Parents, Children and the Search for Identity*. New York: Scribler.

131. Austin, R.D. & Pisano, G. P. (2017) 'Neurodiversity as a competitive advantage: Why you should embrace it in your workforce', *Harvard Business Review*, May-June, 95: 3, pp. 96-103.

132. Wadors, P. (2016) 'Diversity efforts fall short unless employees feel that they belong', *Harvard Business Review Blog*, August 10.

133. McMurtie, B. (2016) 'How to do a better job of searching for diversity', *Chronicle of Higher Education*, September 11. https://www.chronicle.com/article/How-to-Do-a-Better-Job-of/237750

134. Russell, N.S. (2015) *The problem with a trust-but-verify approach*. https://www.psychologytoday.com/blog/trust-the-new-wrkplace-currency/201507/the-problem-trust-but-verify-approach

135. McGregor, D. (1960). *The Human Side of Enterprise*. New York: McGraw-Hill Publishing Company.

136. Russell, N.S (2013) *Trust: Inc: How to Create a Business Culture that will Ignite Passion, Engagement, and Innovation*. Pompton Place: Carer Press.

137. Hinssen, P. (2017) *The Day After Tomorrow: Hoe Overleven in Tijden van Radicale Innovatie*. Leuven: LannooCampus/Van Duuren Management.

138. Long, D. (2105) *Managing Genius: Manage the Art of Managing People*. Lebanon: Franklin Green Publishing.

139. Rockwood, K. (2108) Not-so-human resources. *Inc*, June, http://www.hrtechvalley.org/en/community/map-of-belgian-hr-tech/ enz.

140. Briscoe, D.R., Schuler, R.S. & Claus, L. (1995) *International Human Resource Management: Policies and Practices for Multinational Enterprises*. New York: Routledge.

CHAPTER 7

#ZigZagHR Ecosystem
NO (WO)MAN IS AN ISLAND

141. Hinssen, P. (2017) *The Day After Tomorrow: Hoe Overleven in Tijden van Radicale Innovatie.* Leuven: LannooCampus/Van Duuren Management.

142. Chesbrough, H.M. (2006) *Open innovation: The New Imperative for Creating and Profiting from Technology.* Boston: Harvard Business School Press.

143. https://en.wikipedia.org/wiki/Arthur_Tansley https://en.wikipedia.org/wiki/Eugene_Odum

144. Biomimicricy Nederland – wat is biomimicricy - http://www.biomimicrynl.org/wat-is-biomimicry.html

145. Moore, J. F. (1993) 'Predators and prey: A new ecology of competition', *Harvard Business Review*, May-June, 71: 3, pp. 75-86.

146. Moore, J. F. (1996) The Death of Competition: Leadership and Strategy in the Age of Business Ecosystems, Wiley

147. Ernst, G. & Chrobot-Mason, D. (2011) *Boundary Spanning Leadership: Six Practices for Solving Problems, Driving Innovation, and Transforming Organizations.* New York: McGrah Hill Book company,

148. Geraci, J. (2016) "How an Ecosystem Mindset Can Help People and Organizations Succeed", *Harvard Business Review*, May 12 https://hbr.org/2016/05/how-an-ecosystem-mindset-can-help-people-and-organizations-succeed

149. Harder, H.G., Rash, J. & Wagner, S. et al. (2014) *Mental Illness in the Workplace: Psychological Disability Management.* Gower Publishing.

150. Hinssen, P. (2017) *The Day After Tomorrow: Hoe Overleven in Tijden van Radicale Innovatie.* Leuven: LannooCampus/Van Duuren Management.

151. Govindarajan, V. & Trimble, C. (2011) 'The CEO's role in business model reinvention', *Harvard Business Review*, January-February, 89: 1/2, pp. 108-114.

152. Leslie, M. "The Key to Enduring Growth Is Strategic Transformation" https://www.gsb.stanford.edu/insights/mark-leslie-key-enduring-growth-strategic-transformation (2015)

153. Ansoff, I.H. (1975) Managing Strategic Surprise by Response to Weak Signals, *California Management Review*, 18(2): 21-33.

154. Camp, P. & Erens, F. (1991) *De Gekookte Kikker – 400 Dierenmetaforen over Organisatieverandering*, Amsterdam/Antwerpen, Business Contact pp. 223

155. Staes, J. (2007) Mijn Organisatie Is Een Oerwoud, Lannoo Campus, Mijn Manager Is Een Held (2009), Lannoo Campus, Ik Was Een Schaap (2011), Lannoo Campus.

156. Sarasvathy, S.D. (2001) 'Effectual reasoning in entrepreneurial decision making: Existence and bounds', *Academy of Management Proceedings*, https://www.effectuation.org/wp-content/uploads/2017/05/Effectual-Reasoning-in-Entrepreneurial-Decision-Making-1.pdf

157. Kotter, J. (1995). Leading change: Why transformation efforts fail? *Harvard Business Review*, 73(2): 59-67.

Let's start with the #ZigZagHR-Manifesto

158. Sivers, D. (2010) *How to Start a Movement*. Ted Ideas Worth Spreading https://www.ted.com/talks/derek_sivers_how_to_start_a_movement#t-78988

Index

Made in the USA
Lexington, KY
20 November 2019